UK 2024

NINJA DUAL ZONE Air Fryer

Cookbook for Beginners

Alexandrie Grimard

2000+ Days Easy & Delicious Recipe Book incl. Side Dishes, Snacks, Desserts & More to Satisfy Your Taste Buds | Full-color Edition

Copyright© 2024 By Alexandrie Grimard

All rights reserved worldwide.

No part of this book may be reproduced or transmitted in any form or by any means, electronic or mechanical, including photo- copying, recording or by any information storage and retrieval system, without written permission from the publisher, except for the inclusion of brief quotations in a review.

Warning-Disclaimer

The purpose of this book is to educate and entertain. The author or publisher does not guarantee that anyone following the techniques, suggestions, tips, ideas, or strategies will become successful. The author and publisher shall have neither liability or responsibility to anyone with respect to any loss or damage caused, or alleged to be caused, directly or indirectly by the information contained in this book.

Table of Contents

- 1 / **Introduction**
- 4 / **Chapter 1** — Breakfasts
- 11 / **Chapter 2** — Vegetables and Sides
- 19 / **Chapter 3** — Vegetarian Mains
- 24 / **Chapter 4** — Beef, Pork, and Lamb
- 34 / **Chapter 5** — Fish and Seafood
- 44 / **Chapter 6** — Poultry
- 52 / **Chapter 7** — Snacks and Starters
- 59 / **Chapter 8** — Desserts
- 64 / **Chapter 9** — Family Favorites
- 69 / **Chapter 10** — Fast and Easy Everyday Favourites
- 74 / **Appendix :** Recipes Index

INTRODUCTION

Are you tired of cooking the same old meals every day? Do you want to try something new and exciting in your kitchen? Look no further than the Ninja Dual Zone Air Fryer! With this amazing kitchen appliance, you can cook your favorite foods with little or no oil, resulting in healthier and more delicious meals. From crispy chicken wings to perfectly roasted vegetables, the air fryer can do it all. But don't just take my word for it - try it out for yourself! In my cookbook, I have included a wide range of recipes that showcase the versatility and convenience of the Ninja Dual Zone Air Fryer. From breakfast dishes to desserts, there is something for everyone in this cookbook.

Not only is air frying a healthier alternative to traditional frying methods, but it is also faster and easier. With the air fryer, you can have dinner on the table in no time, without sacrificing taste or quality. So what are you waiting for? Dust off your air fryer and start cooking up a storm! Your taste buds (and waistline) will thank you.

Understanding the Ninja Dual Zone Air Fryer

The Ninja Dual Zone Air Fryer is a kitchen appliance that allows you to cook your favorite foods with little or no oil. It features two separate cooking zones, each with its own temperature and timer controls, allowing you to cook different foods at the same time. The air fryer has a large capacity, capable of holding up to 4 quarts of food, making it perfect for families or entertaining guests. The appliance also comes with a range of accessories, including a crisper plate, a multi-layer rack, and a broil rack, giving you even more versatility in your cooking options. With its easy-to-use digital controls and sleek design, the Ninja Dual Zone Air Fryer is a great addition to any kitchen.

Why Air Frying

Air frying is a cooking method that uses hot air to circulate around food, creating a crispy outer layer without the need for oil. Here are some of the benefits of air frying:

1. Healthier cooking: Air frying reduces the amount of oil needed to cook food, which can result in healthier meals. This is especially beneficial for those who are watching their calorie intake or trying to reduce their fat consumption.

2. Versatility: Air fryers can cook a wide range of foods, from chicken wings and French fries to vegetables and even desserts. They can also be used to reheat leftovers or cook frozen foods, making them a versatile kitchen appliance.

3. Convenience: Air fryers are easy to use and require minimal preparation. Simply season your food, place it in the basket, and set the temperature and time. Many models also come with pre-programmed settings for popular foods.

4. Faster cooking: Air frying can be faster than traditional cooking methods, as the hot air circulates around the food, cooking it evenly and quickly. This means you can have dinner on the table in less time.

5. Easy to clean: Air fryers are generally easy to clean, with many models featuring non-stick baskets that can be removed and washed in the dishwasher.

Overall, air frying is a great way to enjoy crispy, delicious food without the added calories and fat of traditional frying methods.

Tips for Using

Here are the steps to use the Ninja Dual Zone Air Fryer:

1. Place the air fryer on a flat, stable surface and plug it in.
2. Preheat the air fryer by setting the temperature and time for the desired cooking temperature and pressing the "Preheat" button. The preheating process typically takes 3-5 minutes.
3. Prepare your food by seasoning it as desired and placing it in the air fryer basket. You can also use the included accessories, such as the crisper plate or multi-layer rack, to cook multiple items at once.
4. Set the temperature and time for your desired cooking method. The Ninja Dual Zone Air Fryer has two separate cooking zones, so you can set different temperatures and times for each zone if you are cooking multiple items.
5. Press the "Start" button to begin cooking. The air fryer will automatically shut off when the cooking time is complete.
6. Once the cooking is complete, carefully remove the basket from the air fryer and transfer the food to a plate or serving dish.
7. Clean the air fryer basket and accessories according to the manufacturer's instructions.

It is important to note that the specific steps may vary depending on the model of the Ninja Dual Zone Air Fryer you have, so be sure to consult the user manual for detailed instructions.

Cleaning and Maintaining Your Ninja Dual Zone Air Fryer

Proper cleaning and maintenance of your Ninja Dual Zone Air Fryer is important to ensure that it continues to work efficiently and effectively. Here are some tips on how to clean and maintain your air fryer:

1. After each use, allow the air fryer to cool down completely before cleaning.
2. Remove the basket and accessories from the air fryer and wash them with warm soapy water or in the dishwasher.
3. Wipe the interior and exterior of the air fryer with a damp cloth or sponge. Do not use abrasive cleaners or scouring pads as they can damage the non-stick coating.
4. If there is any stubborn food residue or grease buildup, you can use a soft-bristled brush or toothbrush to gently scrub it away.
5. To remove any lingering odors, you can place a few slices of lemon or a tablespoon of baking soda in the basket and run the air fryer at 350°F for 10-15 minutes.
6. Regularly check the heating element and fan for any debris or buildup. You can use a soft-bristled brush or a vacuum cleaner with a brush attachment to remove any dust or debris.
7. Store the air fryer in a dry, cool place when not in use.

By following these simple steps, you can keep your Ninja Dual Zone Air Fryer clean and well-maintained, ensuring that it continues to provide delicious and healthy meals for years to come.

Chapter 1　Breakfasts

Drop Biscuits

Prep time: 10 minutes | Cook time: 9 to 10 minutes | Serves 5

- 500 g plain flour
- 1 tablespoon baking powder
- 1 tablespoon sugar (optional)
- 1 teaspoon salt
- 6 tablespoons butter, plus more for brushing on the biscuits (optional)
- 180 ml buttermilk
- 1 to 2 tablespoons oil

1. In a large bowl, whisk the flour, baking powder, sugar (if using), and salt until blended. 2. Add the butter. Using a pastry cutter or 2 forks, work the dough until pea-size balls of the butter-flour mixture appear. Stir in the buttermilk until the mixture is sticky. 3. Preheat the air fryer to 170ºC. Line the air fryer basket with parchment paper and spritz it with oil. 4. Drop the dough by the tablespoonful onto the prepared basket, leaving 1 inch between each, to form 10 biscuits. 5. In zone 1, select the BAKE button, and set time to 5 minutes. In zone 2, select Match Cook and press Start. Flip the biscuits and cook for 4 minutes more for a light brown top, or 5 minutes more for a darker biscuit. Brush the tops with melted butter, if desired.

Bacon Cheese Egg with Avocado

Prep time: 15 minutes | Cook time: 20 minutes | Serves 4

- 6 large eggs
- 60 ml double cream
- 350 g chopped cauliflower
- 235 g grated medium Cheddar cheese
- 1 medium avocado, peeled and pitted
- 8 tablespoons full-fat sour cream
- 2 spring onions, sliced on the bias
- 12 slices bacon, cooked and crumbled

1. In a medium bowl, whisk eggs and cream together. Pour into a round baking dish. 2. Add cauliflower and mix, then top with Cheddar. Place dish into the air fryer basket. 3. In zone 1, select the AIR FRY button, adjust temperature to 160ºC, set time to 20 minutes. In zone 2, select Match Cook and press Start. 4. When completely cooked, eggs will be firm and cheese will be browned. Slice into four pieces. 5. Slice avocado and divide evenly among pieces. Top each piece with 2 tablespoons sour cream, sliced spring onions, and crumbled bacon.

Bunless Breakfast Turkey Burgers

Prep time: 5 minutes | Cook time: 15 minutes | Serves 4

- 450 g turkey banger meat, removed from casings
- ½ teaspoon salt
- ¼ teaspoon ground black pepper
- 60 g seeded and chopped green pepper
- 2 tablespoons mayonnaise
- 1 medium avocado, peeled, pitted, and sliced

1. In a large bowl, mix banger meat with salt, black pepper, pepper, and mayonnaise. Form meat into four patties. 2. Place patties into ungreased air fryer basket. Adjust the temperature to 190ºC and air fry for 15 minutes, turning patties halfway through cooking. Burgers will be done when dark brown and they have an internal temperature of at least 74ºC. 3. Serve burgers topped with avocado slices on four medium plates.

Keto Quiche

Prep time: 10 minutes | Cook time: 1 hour | Makes 1 (6-inch) quiche

Crust:
- 150 g blanched almond flour
- 300 g grated Parmesan or Gouda cheese
- ¼ teaspoon fine sea salt
- 1 large egg, beaten

Filling:
- 120 g chicken or beef stock (or vegetable stock for vegetarian)
- 235 g grated Swiss cheese (about 110 g)
- 110 g soft cheese (120 ml)
- 1 tablespoon unsalted butter, melted
- 4 large eggs, beaten
- 80 g minced leeks or sliced spring onions
- ¾ teaspoon fine sea salt
- ⅛ teaspoon cayenne pepper
- Chopped spring onions, for garnish

1. Preheat the air fryer to 160ºC. Grease a pie dish. Spray two large pieces of parchment paper with avocado oil and set them on the countertop. 2. Make the crust: In a medium-sized bowl, combine the flour, cheese, and salt and mix well. Add the egg and mix until the dough is well combined and stiff. 3. Place the dough in the center of one of the greased pieces of parchment. Top with the other piece of parchment. Using a rolling pin, roll out the dough into a circle about 1/16 inch thick. 4. Press the pie crust into the prepared pie dish. Place it in the air fryer and bake for 12 minutes, or until it starts to lightly brown. 5. While the crust bakes, make the filling: In a large bowl, combine the stock, Swiss cheese, soft cheese, and butter. Stir in the eggs, leeks, salt, and cayenne pepper. When the crust is ready, pour the mixture into the crust. 6. Place the quiche in the air fryer and bake for 15 minutes. Turn the heat down to 150ºC and bake for an additional 30 minutes, or until a knife inserted 1 inch from the edge comes out clean. You may have to cover the edges of the crust with foil to prevent burning. 7. Allow the quiche to cool for 10 minutes before garnishing it with chopped spring onions and cutting it into wedges. 8. Store leftovers in an airtight container in the refrigerator for up to 4 days or in the freezer for up to a month. Reheat in a preheated 180ºC air fryer for a few minutes, until warmed through.

Chimichanga Breakfast Burrito

Prep time: 10 minutes | Cook time: 10 minutes | Serves 2

- 2 large (10- to 12-inch) wheat maize wraps
- 120 g canned refried beans (pinto or black work equally well)
- 4 large eggs, cooked scrambled
- 4 maize maize wrap chips, crushed
- 120 g grated chilli cheese
- 12 pickled jalapeño slices
- 1 tablespoon vegetable oil
- Guacamole, tomato salsa, and sour cream, for serving (optional)

1. Place the maize wraps on a work surface and divide the refried beans between them, spreading them in a rough rectangle in the center of the maize wraps. Top the beans with the scrambled eggs, crushed chips, cheese, and jalapeños. Fold one side over the fillings, then fold in each short side and roll up the rest of the way like a burrito. 2. Brush the outside of the burritos with the oil, then transfer to the air fryer, seam-side down. Air fry at 180ºC until the maize wraps are browned and crisp and the filling is warm throughout, about 10 minutes. 3. Transfer the chimichangas to plates and serve warm with guacamole, tomato salsa, and sour cream, if you like.

Berry Muffins

Prep time: 15 minutes | Cook time: 12 to 17 minutes | Makes 8 muffins

- 160 g plus 1 tablespoon plain flour, divided
- 48 g granulated sugar
- 2 tablespoons light soft brown sugar
- 2 teaspoons baking powder
- 2 eggs
- 160 ml whole milk
- 80 ml neutral oil
- 235 g mixed fresh berries

1. In a medium bowl, stir together 315 g of flour, the granulated sugar, soft brown sugar, and baking powder until mixed well. 2. In a small bowl, whisk the eggs, milk, and oil until combined. Stir the egg mixture into the dry ingredients just until combined. 3. In another small bowl, toss the mixed berries with the remaining 1 tablespoon of flour until coated. Gently stir the berries into the batter. 4. Double up 16 foil muffin cups to make 8 cups. 5. Insert the crisper plate into the basket and the basket into the unit. Preheat the unit by selecting BAKE, setting the temperature to 160ºC, and setting the time to 3 minutes. Select START/STOP to begin. 6. Once the unit is preheated, place 1 L into the basket and fill each three-quarters full with the batter. 7. Select BAKE, set the temperature to 160ºC, and set the time for 17 minutes. Select START/STOP to begin. 8. After about 12 minutes, check the muffins. If they spring back when lightly touched with your finger, they are done. If not, resume cooking. 9. When the cooking is done, transfer the muffins to a wire rack to cool. 10. Repeat steps 6, 7, and 8 with the remaining muffin cups and batter. 11. Let the muffins cool for 10 minutes before serving.

Three-Berry Dutch Pancake

Prep time: 10 minutes | Cook time: 12 to 16 minutes | Serves 4

- 2 egg whites
- 1 egg
- 60 g wholemeal plain flour plus 1 tablespoon cornflour
- 120 ml semi-skimmed milk
- 1 teaspoon pure vanilla extract
- 1 tablespoon unsalted butter, melted
- 235 g sliced fresh strawberries
- 120 g fresh blueberries
- 120 g fresh raspberries

1. In a medium bowl, use an eggbeater or hand mixer to quickly mix the egg whites, egg, flour, milk, and vanilla until well combined. 2. Use a pastry brush to grease the bottom of a baking pan with the melted butter. Immediately pour in the batter and put the basket back in the fryer. In zone 1, select the BAKE button, adjust temperature to 170ºC, set time to 12 to 16 minutes, or until the pancake is puffed and golden brown. In zone 2, select Match Cook and press Start. 3. Remove the pan from the air fryer; the pancake will fall. Top with the strawberries, blueberries, and raspberries. Serve immediately.

Pizza Eggs

Prep time: 5 minutes | Cook time: 10 minutes | Serves 2

- 235 g grated Cheddar cheese
- 7 slices pepperoni, chopped
- 1 large egg, whisked
- ¼ teaspoon dried oregano
- ¼ teaspoon dried parsley
- ¼ teaspoon garlic powder
- ¼ teaspoon salt

1. Place Mozzarella in a single layer on the bottom of an ungreased round nonstick baking dish. Scatter pepperoni over cheese, then pour egg evenly around baking dish. 2. Sprinkle with remaining ingredients and place into air fryer basket. In zone 1, select the BAKE button, adjust temperature to 170ºC, set time to 10 minutes. In zone 2, select Match Cook and press Start. When cheese is brown and egg is set, dish will be done. 3. Let cool in dish 5 minutes before serving.

Cheddar Eggs

Prep time: 5 minutes | Cook time: 15 minutes | Serves 2

- 4 large eggs
- 2 tablespoons unsalted butter, melted
- 120 g grated mature Cheddar cheese

1. Crack eggs into a round baking dish and whisk. Place dish into the air fryer basket. 2. Adjust the temperature to 200ºC and set the timer for 10 minutes. 3. After 5 minutes, stir the eggs and add the butter and cheese. Let cook 3 more minutes and stir again. 4. Allow eggs to finish cooking an additional 2 minutes or remove if they are to your desired liking. 5. Use a fork to fluff. Serve warm.

Mozzarella Bacon Calzones

Prep time: 15 minutes | Cook time: 12 minutes | Serves 4

- 2 large eggs
- 120 g blanched finely ground almond flour
- 475 g grated Cheddar cheese
- 60 g soft cheese, softened and broken into small pieces
- 4 slices cooked bacon, crumbled

1. Beat eggs in a small bowl. Pour into a medium nonstick frying pan over medium heat and scramble. Set aside. 2. In a large microwave-safe bowl, mix flour and Mozzarella. Add soft cheese to the bowl. 3. Place bowl in microwave and cook 45 seconds on high to melt cheese, then stir with a fork until a soft dough ball forms. 4. Cut a piece of parchment to fit air fryer basket. Separate dough into two sections and press each out into an 8-inch round. 5. On half of each dough round, place half of the scrambled eggs and crumbled bacon. Fold the other side of the dough over and press to seal the edges. 6. Place calzones on ungreased parchment and into air fryer basket. Adjust the temperature to 180ºC and set the timer for 12 minutes, turning calzones halfway through cooking. Crust will be golden and firm when done. 7. Let calzones cool on a cooking rack 5 minutes before serving.

Egg in a Hole

Prep time: 5 minutes | Cook time: 5 minutes | Serves 1

- 1 slice bread
- 1 teaspoon butter, softened
- 1 egg
- Salt and pepper, to taste
- 1 tablespoon grated Cheddar cheese
- 2 teaspoons diced gammon

1. Preheat the air fryer to 170ºC. Place a baking dish in the air fryer basket. 2. On a flat work surface, cut a hole in the center of the bread slice with a 2½-inch-diameter biscuit cutter. 3. Spread the butter evenly on each side of the bread slice and transfer to the baking dish. 4. Crack the egg into the hole and season as desired with salt and pepper. Scatter the grated cheese and diced gammon on top. 5. Bake in the preheated air fryer for 5 minutes until the bread is lightly browned and the egg is cooked to your preference. 6. Remove from the basket and serve hot.

Apple Rolls

Prep time: 20 minutes | Cook time: 20 to 24 minutes | Makes 12 rolls

Apple Rolls:
- 235 g plain flour, plus more for dusting
- 2 tablespoons granulated sugar
- 1 teaspoon salt
- 3 tablespoons butter, at room temperature
- 180 ml milk, whole or semi-skimmed

Icing:
- 75 g icing sugar
- ½ teaspoon vanilla extract
- 95 g packed light soft brown sugar
- 1 teaspoon ground cinnamon
- 1 large Granny Smith apple, peeled and diced
- 1 to 2 tablespoons oil

- 2 to 3 tablespoons milk, whole or semi-skimmed

Make the Apple Rolls: 1. In a large bowl, whisk the flour, granulated sugar, and salt until blended. Stir in the butter and milk briefly until a sticky dough forms. 2. In a small bowl, stir together the soft brown sugar, cinnamon, and apple. 3. Place a piece of parchment paper on a work surface and dust it with flour. Roll the dough on the prepared surface to ¼ inch thickness. 4. Spread the apple mixture over the dough. Roll up the dough jam roll-style, pinching the ends to seal. Cut the dough into 12 rolls. 5. Preheat the air fryer to 160ºC. 6. Line the air fryer basket with parchment paper and spritz it with oil. Place 6 rolls on the prepared parchment. 7. In zone 1, select the BAKE button, and set time to 5 minutes. In zone 2, select Match Cook and press Start. Flip the rolls and bake for 5 to 7 minutes more until lightly browned. Repeat with the remaining rolls. Make the Icing 8. In a medium bowl, whisk the icing sugar, vanilla, and milk until blended. 9. Drizzle over the warm rolls.

Spinach and Swiss Frittata with Mushrooms

Prep time: 10 minutes | Cook time: 20 minutes | Serves 4

- rapeseed oil cooking spray
- 8 large eggs
- ½ teaspoon salt
- ½ teaspoon black pepper
- 1 garlic clove, minced
- 475 g fresh baby spinach
- 110 g baby mushrooms, sliced
- 1 shallot, diced
- 120 g grated Swiss cheese, divided
- Hot sauce, for serving (optional)

1. Preheat the air fryer to 180ºC. Lightly coat the inside of a 6-inch round cake pan with rapeseed oil cooking spray. 2. In a large bowl, beat the eggs, salt, pepper, and garlic for 1 to 2 minutes, or until well combined. 3. Fold in the spinach, mushrooms, shallot, and 60 ml the Swiss cheese. 4. Pour the egg mixture into the prepared cake pan, and sprinkle the remaining 60 ml Swiss over the top. 5. In zone 1, select the BAKE button, and set time to 18 to 20 minutes or until the eggs are set in the center. In zone 2, select Match Cook and press Start. 6. Remove from the air fryer and allow to cool for 5 minutes. Drizzle with hot sauce (if using) before serving.

Meritage Eggs

Prep time: 5 minutes | Cook time: 8 minutes | Serves 2

- 2 teaspoons unsalted butter (or coconut oil for dairy-free), for greasing the ramekins
- 4 large eggs
- 2 teaspoons chopped fresh thyme
- ½ teaspoon fine sea salt
- ¼ teaspoon ground black pepper
- 2 tablespoons double cream (or unsweetened, unflavoured almond milk for dairy-free)
- 3 tablespoons finely grated Parmesan cheese (or chive soft cheese style spread, softened, for dairy-free)
- Fresh thyme leaves, for garnish (optional)

1. Preheat the air fryer to 200ºC. Grease two (110 g) ramekins with the butter. 2. Crack 2 eggs into each ramekin and divide the thyme, salt, and pepper between the ramekins. Pour 1 tablespoon of the double cream into each ramekin. Sprinkle each ramekin with 1½ tablespoons of the Parmesan cheese. 3. Place the ramekins in the air fryer. In zone 1, select the BAKE button, and set time to 8 minutes for soft-cooked yolks (longer if you desire a harder yolk). In zone 2, select Match Cook and press Start. 4. Garnish with a sprinkle of ground black pepper and thyme leaves, if desired. Best served fresh.

Chapter 2 Vegetables and Sides

Cheesy Loaded Broccoli

Prep time: 10 minutes | Cook time: 10 minutes | Serves 2

- 215 g fresh broccoli florets
- 1 tablespoon coconut oil
- ¼ teaspoon salt
- 120 g shredded sharp Cheddar cheese
- 60 g sour cream
- 4 slices cooked sugar-free bacon, crumbled
- 1 medium spring onion, trimmed and sliced on the bias

1. Place broccoli into ungreased air fryer basket, drizzle with coconut oil, and sprinkle with salt. In zone 1, select the ROAST button, adjust temperature to 180ºC, set time to 8 minutes. In zone 2, select Match Cook and press Start. Shake basket three times during cooking to avoid burned spots. 2. Sprinkle broccoli with Cheddar and cook for 2 additional minutes. When done, cheese will be melted and broccoli will be tender. 3. Serve warm in a large serving dish, topped with sour cream, crumbled bacon, and spring onion slices.

Banger-Stuffed Mushroom Caps

Prep time: 10 minutes | Cook time: 8 minutes | Serves 2

- 6 large portobello mushroom caps
- 230 g Italian banger
- 15 g chopped onion
- 2 tablespoons blanched finely ground almond flour
- 20 g grated Parmesan cheese
- 1 teaspoon minced fresh garlic

1. Use a spoon to hollow out each mushroom cap, reserving scrapings. 2. In a medium frying pan over medium heat, brown the banger about 10 minutes or until fully cooked and no pink remains. Drain and then add reserved mushroom scrapings, onion, almond flour, Parmesan, and garlic. Gently fold ingredients together and continue cooking an additional minute, then remove from heat. 3. Evenly spoon the mixture into mushroom caps and place the caps into a 6-inch round pan. Place pan into the air fryer basket. 4. In zone 1, select the AIR FRY button, adjust temperature to 190ºC, set time to 8 minutes. In zone 2, select Match Cook and press Start. 5. When finished cooking, the tops will be browned and bubbling. Serve warm.

Spinach and Sweet Pepper Poppers

Prep time: 10 minutes | Cook time: 8 minutes | Makes 16 poppers

- 110 g cream cheese, softened
- 20 g chopped fresh spinach leaves
- ½ teaspoon garlic powder
- 8 mini sweet peppers, tops removed, seeded, and halved lengthwise

1. In a medium bowl, mix cream cheese, spinach, and garlic powder. Place 1 tablespoon mixture into each sweet pepper half and press down to smooth. 2. Place poppers into ungreased air fryer basket. In zone 1, select the AIR FRY button, adjust temperature to 200ºC, set time to 8 minutes. In zone 2, select Match Cook and press Start. Poppers will be done when cheese is browned on top and peppers are tender-crisp. Serve warm.

Parmesan Herb Focaccia Bread

Prep time: 10 minutes | Cook time: 10 minutes | Serves 6

- 225 g shredded Mozzarella cheese
- 30 g full-fat cream cheese
- 95 g blanched finely ground almond flour
- 40 g ground golden flaxseed
- 20 g grated Parmesan cheese
- ½ teaspoon bicarbonate of soda
- 2 large eggs
- ½ teaspoon garlic powder
- ¼ teaspoon dried basil
- ¼ teaspoon dried rosemary
- 2 tablespoons salted butter, melted and divided

1. Place Mozzarella, cream cheese, and almond flour into a large microwave-safe bowl and microwave for 1 minute. Add the flaxseed, Parmesan, and bicarbonate of soda and stir until smooth ball forms. If the mixture cools too much, it will be hard to mix. Return to microwave for 10 to 15 seconds to rewarm if necessary. 2. Stir in eggs. You may need to use your hands to get them fully incorporated. Just keep stirring and they will absorb into the dough. 3. Sprinkle dough with garlic powder, basil, and rosemary and knead into dough. Grease a baking pan with 1 tablespoon melted butter. Press the dough evenly into the pan. Place pan into the air fryer basket. 4. In zone 1, select the BAKE button, adjust temperature to 200ºC, set time to 10 minutes. In zone 2, select Match Cook and press Start. 5. At 7 minutes, cover with foil if bread begins to get too dark. 6. Remove and let cool at least 30 minutes. Drizzle with remaining butter and serve.

Shishito Pepper Roast

Prep time: 4 minutes | Cook time: 9 minutes | Serves 4

- Cooking oil spray (sunflower, safflower, or refined coconut)
- 450 g shishito, Anaheim, or peppers, rinsed
- 1 tablespoon soy sauce
- 2 teaspoons freshly squeezed lime juice
- 2 large garlic cloves, pressed

1. Insert the crisper plate into the basket and the basket into the unit. Preheat the unit by selecting ROAST, setting the temperature to 200ºC, and setting the time to 3 minutes. Select START/STOP to begin. 2. Once the unit is preheated, spray the crisper plate and the basket with cooking oil. Place the peppers into the basket and spray them with oil. 3. In zone 1, select the ROAST button, adjust temperature to 200ºC, set time to 9 minutes. In zone 2, select Match Cook and press Start. 4. After 3 minutes, remove the basket and shake the peppers. Spray the peppers with more oil. Reinsert the basket to resume cooking. Repeat this step again after 3 minutes. 5. While the peppers roast, in a medium bowl, whisk the soy sauce, lime juice, and garlic until combined. Set aside. 6. When the cooking is complete, several of the peppers should have lots of nice browned spots on them. If using Anaheim or peppers, cut a slit in the side of each pepper and remove the seeds, which tin be bitter. 7. Place the roasted peppers in the bowl with the sauce. Toss to coat the peppers evenly and serve.

Parmesan and Herb Sweet Potatoes

Prep time: 10 minutes | Cook time: 18 minutes | Serves 4

- 2 large sweet potatoes, peeled and cubed
- 65 ml olive oil
- 1 teaspoon dried rosemary
- ½ teaspoon salt
- 2 tablespoons shredded Parmesan

1. Preheat the air fryer to 180ºC. 2. In a large bowl, toss the sweet potatoes with the olive oil, rosemary, and salt. 3. Pour the potatoes into the air fryer basket. In zone 1, select the ROAST button, and set time to 10 minutes. In zone 2, select Match Cook and press Start. Then stir the potatoes and sprinkle the Parmesan over the top. Continue roasting for 8 minutes more. 4. Serve hot and enjoy.

Glazed Carrots

Prep time: 10 minutes | Cook time: 8 to 10 minutes | Serves 4

- 2 teaspoons honey
- 1 teaspoon orange juice
- ½ teaspoon grated orange rind
- ⅛ teaspoon ginger
- 450 g baby carrots
- 2 teaspoons olive oil
- ¼ teaspoon salt

1. Combine honey, orange juice, grated rind, and ginger in a small bowl and set aside. 2. Toss the carrots, oil, and salt together to coat well and pour them into the air fryer basket. 3. In zone 1, select the ROAST button, adjust temperature to 200ºC, set time to 5 minutes. In zone 2, select Match Cook and press Start. Shake basket to stir a little and cook for 2 to 4 minutes more, until carrots are barely tender. 4. Pour carrots into a baking pan. 5. Stir the honey mixture to combine well, pour glaze over carrots, and stir to coat. 6. Roast at 180ºC for 1 minute or just until heated through.

Garlic-Parmesan Crispy Baby Potatoes

Prep time: 10 minutes | Cook time: 15 minutes | Serves 4

- Oil, for spraying
- 450 g baby potatoes
- 45 g grated Parmesan cheese, divided
- 3 tablespoons olive oil
- 2 teaspoons garlic powder
- ½ teaspoon onion powder
- ½ teaspoon salt
- ¼ teaspoon freshly ground black pepper
- ¼ teaspoon paprika
- 2 tablespoons chopped fresh parsley, for garnish

1. Line the air fryer basket with parchment and spray lightly with oil. 2. Rinse the potatoes, pat dry with paper towels, and place in a large bowl. 3. In a small bowl, mix together 45 g of Parmesan cheese, the olive oil, garlic, onion powder, salt, black pepper, and paprika. Pour the mixture over the potatoes and toss to coat. 4. Transfer the potatoes to the prepared basket and spread them out in an even layer, taking care to keep them from touching. 5. In zone 1, select the AIR FRY button, adjust temperature to 200ºC, set time to 15 minutes. In zone 2, select Match Cook and press Start, stirring after 7 to 8 minutes, or until easily pierced with a fork. Continue to cook for another 1 to 2 minutes, if needed. 6. Sprinkle with the parsley and the remaining Parmesan cheese and serve.

Caramelized Aubergine with Harissa Yoghurt

Prep time: 10 minutes | Cook time: 15 minutes | Serves 2

- 1 medium aubergine (about 340 g), cut crosswise into ½-inch-thick slices and quartered
- 2 tablespoons vegetable oil
- coarse sea salt and freshly ground black pepper, to taste
- 120 g plain yoghurt (not Greek)
- 2 tablespoons harissa paste
- 1 garlic clove, grated
- 2 teaspoons honey

1. In a bowl, toss together the aubergine and oil, season with salt and pepper, and toss to coat evenly. In zone 1, select the AIR FRY button, adjust temperature to 200ºC, set time to 15 minutes until the aubergine is caramelized and tender. In zone 2, select Match Cook and press Start, shaking the basket every 5 minutes. 2. Meanwhile, in a small bowl, whisk together the yoghurt, harissa, and garlic, then spread onto a serving plate. 3. Pile the warm aubergine over the yoghurt and drizzle with the honey just before serving.

Fried Brussels Sprouts

Prep time: 10 minutes | Cook time: 18 minutes | Serves 4

- 1 teaspoon plus 1 tablespoon extra-virgin olive oil, divided
- 2 teaspoons minced garlic
- 2 tablespoons honey
- 1 tablespoon sugar
- 2 tablespoons freshly squeezed lemon juice
- 2 tablespoons rice vinegar
- 2 tablespoons sriracha
- 450 g Brussels sprouts, stems trimmed and any tough leaves removed, rinsed, halved lengthwise, and dried
- ½ teaspoon salt
- Cooking oil spray

1. In a small saucepan over low heat, combine 1 teaspoon of olive oil, the garlic, honey, sugar, lemon juice, vinegar, and sriracha. Cook for 2 to 3 minutes, or until slightly thickened. Remove the pan from the heat, cover, and set aside. 2. Place the Brussels sprouts in a resealable bag or small bowl. Add the remaining olive oil and the salt, and toss to coat. 3. Insert the crisper plate into the basket and the basket into the unit. Preheat the unit by selecting AIR FRY, setting the temperature to 200ºC, and setting the time to 3 minutes. Select START/STOP to begin. 4. Once the unit is preheated, spray the crisper plate with cooking oil. Add the Brussels sprouts to the basket. 5. In zone 1, select the AIR FRY button, adjust temperature to 200ºC, set time to 15 minutes. In zone 2, select Match Cook and press Start. 6. After 7 or 8 minutes, remove the basket and shake it to toss the sprouts. Reinsert the basket to resume cooking. 7. When the cooking is complete, the leaves should be crispy and light brown and the sprout centres tender. 8. Place the sprouts in a medium serving bowl and drizzle the sauce over the top. Toss to coat, and serve immediately.

Tahini-Lemon Kale

Prep time: 5 minutes | Cook time: 15 minutes | Serves 2 to 4

- 60 g tahini
- 60 g fresh lemon juice
- 2 tablespoons olive oil
- 1 teaspoon sesame seeds
- ½ teaspoon garlic powder
- ¼ teaspoon cayenne pepper
- 110 g packed torn kale leaves (stems and ribs removed and leaves torn into palm-size pieces)
- coarse sea salt and freshly ground black pepper, to taste

1. In a large bowl, whisk together the tahini, lemon juice, olive oil, sesame seeds, garlic powder, and cayenne until smooth. Add the kale leaves, season with salt and black pepper, and toss in the dressing until completely coated. Transfer the kale leaves to a cake pan. 2. Place the pan in the air fryer and roast at 180ºC, stirring every 5 minutes, until the kale is wilted and the top is lightly browned, about 15 minutes. Remove the pan from the air fryer and serve warm.

Asian Tofu Salad

Prep time: 25 minutes | Cook time: 15 minutes | Serves 2

Tofu:
- 1 tablespoon soy sauce
- 1 tablespoon vegetable oil
- 1 teaspoon minced fresh ginger

Salad:
- 60 ml rice vinegar
- 1 tablespoon sugar
- 1 teaspoon salt
- 1 teaspoon black pepper
- 25 g sliced spring onions
- 1 teaspoon minced garlic
- 230 g extra-firm tofu, drained and cubed
- 120 g julienned cucumber
- 50 g julienned red onion
- 130 g julienned carrots
- 6 butter lettuce leaves

1. For the tofu: In a small bowl, whisk together the soy sauce, vegetable oil, ginger, and garlic. Add the tofu and mix gently. Let stand at room temperature for 10 minutes. 2. Arrange the tofu in a single layer in the air fryer basket. In zone 1, select the AIR FRY button, adjust temperature to 200ºC, set time to 15 minutes. In zone 2, select Match Cook and press Start, shaking halfway through the cooking time. 3. Meanwhile, for the salad: In a large bowl, whisk together the vinegar, sugar, salt, pepper, and spring onions. Add the cucumber, onion, and carrots and toss to combine. Set aside to marinate while the tofu cooks. 4. To serve, arrange three lettuce leaves on each of two plates. Pile the marinated vegetables (and marinade) on the lettuce. Divide the tofu between the plates and serve.

Butter and Garlic Fried Cabbage

Prep time: 5 minutes | Cook time: 9 minutes | Serves 2

- Oil, for spraying
- ½ head cabbage, cut into bite-size pieces
- 2 tablespoons unsalted butter, melted
- 1 teaspoon granulated garlic
- ½ teaspoon coarse sea salt
- ¼ teaspoon freshly ground black pepper

1. Line the air fryer basket with parchment and spray lightly with oil. 2. In a large bowl, mix together the cabbage, butter, garlic, salt, and black pepper until evenly coated. 3. Transfer the cabbage to the prepared basket and spray lightly with oil. 4. In zone 1, select the AIR FRY button, adjust temperature to 190ºC, set time to 5 minutes. In zone 2, select Match Cook and press Start. Toss, and cook for another 3 to 4 minutes, or until lightly crispy.

Herbed Shiitake Mushrooms

Prep time: 10 minutes | Cook time: 5 minutes | Serves 4

- 230 g shiitake mushrooms, stems removed and caps roughly chopped
- 1 tablespoon olive oil
- ½ teaspoon salt
- Freshly ground black pepper, to taste
- 1 teaspoon chopped fresh thyme leaves
- 1 teaspoon chopped fresh oregano
- 1 tablespoon chopped fresh parsley

1. Preheat the air fryer to 200ºC. 2. Toss the mushrooms with the olive oil, salt, pepper, thyme and oregano. In zone 1, select the AIR FRY button, and set time to 5 minutes. In zone 2, select Match Cook and press Start. , shaking the basket once or twice during the cooking process. The mushrooms will still be somewhat chewy with a meaty texture. If you'd like them a little more tender, add a couple of minutes to this cooking time. 3. Once cooked, add the parsley to the mushrooms and toss. Season again to taste and serve.

Garlic and Thyme Tomatoes

Prep time: 10 minutes | Cook time: 15 minutes | Serves 2 to 4

- 4 plum tomatoes
- 1 tablespoon olive oil
- Salt and freshly ground black pepper, to taste
- 1 clove garlic, minced
- ½ teaspoon dried thyme

1. Preheat the air fryer to 200ºC. 2. Cut the tomatoes in half and scoop out the seeds and any pithy parts with your fingers. Place the tomatoes in a bowl and toss with the olive oil, salt, pepper, garlic and thyme. 3. Transfer the tomatoes to the air fryer, cut side up. In zone 1, select the AIR FRY button, and set time to 15 minutes. In zone 2, select Match Cook and press Start. The edges should just start to brown. Let the tomatoes cool to an edible temperature for a few minutes and then use in pastas, on top of crostini, or as an accompaniment to any poultry, meat or fish.

Citrus-Roasted Broccoli Florets

Prep time: 5 minutes | Cook time: 12 minutes | Serves 6

- 285 g broccoli florets (approximately 1 large head)
- 2 tablespoons olive oil
- ½ teaspoon salt
- 130 ml orange juice
- 1 tablespoon raw honey
- Orange wedges, for serving (optional)

1. Preheat the air fryer to 180ºC. 2. In a large bowl, combine the broccoli, olive oil, salt, orange juice, and honey. Toss the broccoli in the liquid until well coated. 3. Pour the broccoli mixture into the air fryer basket. In zone 1, select the ROAST button, and set time to 6 minutes. In zone 2, select Match Cook and press Start. Stir and roast for 6 minutes more. 4. Serve alone or with orange wedges for additional citrus flavour, if desired.

Chapter 3 Vegetarian Mains

Roasted Vegetable Mélange with Herbs

Prep time: 10 minutes | Cook time: 14 to 18 minutes | Serves 4

- 1 (230 g) package sliced mushrooms
- 1 yellow butternut marrow, sliced
- 1 red pepper, sliced
- 3 cloves garlic, sliced
- 1 tablespoon olive oil
- ½ teaspoon dried basil
- ½ teaspoon dried thyme
- ½ teaspoon dried tarragon

1. Preheat the air fryer to 180ºC. 2.Toss the mushrooms, marrow, and pepper with the garlic and olive oil in a large bowl until well coated. 3.Mix in the basil, thyme, and tarragon and toss again. 4.Spread the vegetables evenly in the air fryer basket. In zone 1, select the ROAST button, and set time to 14 to 18 minutes, or until the vegetables are fork-tender. . In zone 2, select Match Cook and press Start.5.Cool for 5 minutes before serving.

Roasted Vegetables with Rice

Prep time: 5 minutes | Cook time: 12 minutes | Serves 4

- 2 teaspoons melted butter
- 235 g chopped mushrooms
- 235 g cooked rice
- 235 g peas
- 1 carrot, chopped
- 1 red onion, chopped
- 1 garlic clove, minced
- Salt and black pepper, to taste
- 2 hard-boiled eggs, grated
- 1 tablespoon soy sauce

1. Preheat the air fryer to 190ºC. 2.Coat a baking dish with melted butter. 3.Stir together the mushrooms, cooked rice, peas, carrot, onion, garlic, salt, and pepper in a large bowl until well mixed. 4.Pour the mixture into the prepared baking dish and transfer to the air fryer basket. 5.Roast in the preheated air fryer for 12 minutes until the vegetables are tender. 6.Divide the mixture among four plates. 7.Serve warm with a sprinkle of grated eggs and a drizzle of soy sauce.

Teriyaki Cauliflower

Prep time: 5 minutes | Cook time: 14 minutes | Serves 4

- 120 ml soy sauce
- 80 ml water
- 1 tablespoon brown sugar
- 1 teaspoon sesame oil
- 1 teaspoon cornflour
- 2 cloves garlic, chopped
- ½ teaspoon chilli powder
- 1 big cauliflower head, cut into florets

1. Preheat the air fryer to 170ºC. 2.Make the teriyaki sauce: In a small bowl, whisk together the soy sauce, water, brown sugar, sesame oil, cornflour, garlic, and chilli powder until well combined. 3.Place the cauliflower florets in a large bowl and drizzle the top with the prepared teriyaki sauce and toss to coat well. 4.Put the cauliflower florets in the air fryer basket. In zone 1, select the AIR FRY button, and set time to 14 minutes. In zone 2, select Match Cook and press Start, shaking the basket halfway through, or until the cauliflower is crisp-tender. 5.Let the cauliflower cool for 5 minutes before serving.

Crispy Aubergine Rounds

Prep time: 15 minutes | Cook time: 10 minutes | Serves 4

- 1 large aubergine, ends trimmed, cut into ½-inch slices
- ½ teaspoon salt
- 60 g Parmesan 100% cheese crisps, finely ground
- ½ teaspoon paprika
- ¼ teaspoon garlic powder
- 1 large egg

1. Sprinkle aubergine rounds with salt. 2.Place rounds on a kitchen towel for 30 minutes to draw out excess water. 3.Pat rounds dry. 4.In a medium bowl, mix cheese crisps, paprika, and garlic powder. 5.In a separate medium bowl, whisk egg. 6.Dip each aubergine round in egg, then gently press into cheese crisps to coat both sides. 7.Place aubergine rounds into ungreased air fryer basket. 8. In zone 1, select the AIR FRY button, adjust temperature to 200ºC, set time to 10 minutes. In zone 2, select Match Cook and press Start, turning rounds halfway through cooking. 9.Aubergine will be golden and crispy when done. 10.Serve warm.

Mediterranean Pan Pizza

Prep time: 5 minutes | Cook time: 8 minutes | Serves 2

- 235 g shredded Mozzarella cheese
- ¼ medium red pepper, seeded and chopped
- 120 g chopped fresh spinach leaves
- 2 tablespoons chopped black olives
- 2 tablespoons crumbled feta cheese

1. Sprinkle Mozzarella into an ungreased round non-stick baking dish in an even layer. 2. Add remaining ingredients on top. 3. Place dish into air fryer basket. 4. In zone 1, select the BAKE button, adjust temperature to 180ºC, set time to 8 minutes. In zone 2, select Match Cook and press Start, checking halfway through to avoid burning. 5. Top of pizza will be golden brown, and the cheese melted when done. 6. Remove dish from fryer and let cool 5 minutes before slicing and serving.

Stuffed Portobellos

Prep time: 10 minutes | Cook time: 8 minutes | Serves 4

- 85 g soft white cheese
- ½ medium courgette, trimmed and chopped
- 60 g seeded and chopped red pepper
- 350 g chopped fresh spinach leaves
- 4 large portobello mushrooms, stems removed
- 2 tablespoons coconut oil, melted
- ½ teaspoon salt

1. In a medium bowl, mix soft white cheese, courgette, pepper, and spinach. 2. Drizzle mushrooms with coconut oil and sprinkle with salt. 3. Scoop ¼ courgette mixture into each mushroom. 4. Place mushrooms into ungreased air fryer basket. 5. In zone 1, select the AIR FRY button, adjust temperature to 200ºC, set time to 8 minutes. In zone 2, select Match Cook and press Start. 6. Portobellos will be tender, and tops will be browned when done. 7. Serve warm.

Greek Stuffed Aubergine

Prep time: 15 minutes | Cook time: 20 minutes | Serves 2

- 1 large aubergine
- 2 tablespoons unsalted butter
- ¼ medium brown onion, diced
- 60 g chopped artichoke hearts
- 235 g fresh spinach
- 2 tablespoons diced red pepper
- 120 g crumbled feta

1. Slice aubergine in half lengthwise and scoop out flesh, leaving enough inside for shell to remain intact. 2. Take aubergine that was scooped out, chop it, and set aside. In a medium frying pan over medium heat, add butter and onion. 3. Sauté until onions begin to soften, about 3 to 5 minutes. Add chopped aubergine, artichokes, spinach, and pepper. 4. Continue cooking 5 minutes until peppers soften and spinach wilts. Remove from the heat and gently fold in the feta. 5. Place filling into each aubergine shell and place into the air fryer basket. 6. In zone 1, select the AIR FRY button, adjust temperature to 160ºC, set time to 20 minutes. In zone 2, select Match Cook and press Start. 7. Aubergine will be tender when done. 8. Serve warm.

Loaded Cauliflower Steak

Prep time: 5 minutes | Cook time: 7 minutes | Serves 4

- 1 medium head cauliflower
- 60 ml hot sauce
- 2 tablespoons salted butter, melted
- 60 g blue cheese, crumbled
- 60 g full-fat ranch dressing

1. Remove cauliflower leaves. Slice the head in ½-inch-thick slices. In a small bowl, mix hot sauce and butter. Brush the mixture over the cauliflower. 2. Place each cauliflower steak into the air fryer, working in batches if necessary. 3. In zone 1, select the AIR FRY button, adjust temperature to 200ºC, set time to 7 minutes. In zone 2, select Match Cook and press Start. 4. When cooked, edges will begin turning dark and caramelized. To serve, sprinkle steaks with crumbled blue cheese. 5. Drizzle with ranch dressing.

Cheese Stuffed Courgette

Prep time: 20 minutes | Cook time: 8 minutes | Serves 4

- 1 large courgette, cut into four pieces
- 2 tablespoons olive oil
- 235 g Ricotta cheese, room temperature
- 2 tablespoons spring onions, chopped
- 1 heaping tablespoon fresh parsley, roughly chopped
- 1 heaping tablespoon coriander, minced
- 60 g Cheddar cheese, preferably freshly grated
- 1 teaspoon celery seeds
- ½ teaspoon salt
- ½ teaspoon garlic pepper

1. In zone 1, select the AIR FRY button, adjust temperature to 180°C, set time to 10 minutes. In zone 2, select Match Cook and press Start. 2. Check for doneness and cook for 2-3 minutes longer if needed. 3. Meanwhile, make the stuffing by mixing the other items. 4. When your courgette is thoroughly cooked, open them up. 5. Divide the stuffing among all courgette pieces and bake an additional 5 minutes.

Caprese Aubergine Stacks

Prep time: 5 minutes | Cook time: 12 minutes | Serves 4

- 1 medium aubergine, cut into ¼-inch slices
- 2 large tomatoes, cut into ¼-inch slices
- 110 g fresh Mozzarella, cut into 14 g slices
- 2 tablespoons olive oil
- 60 g fresh basil, sliced

1. In a baking dish, place four slices of aubergine on the bottom. 2. Place a slice of tomato on top of each aubergine round, then Mozzarella, then aubergine. 3. Repeat as necessary. 4. Drizzle with olive oil. 5. Cover dish with foil and place dish into the air fryer basket. 6. In zone 1, select the BAKE button, adjust temperature to 180°C, set time to 12 minutes. In zone 2, select Match Cook and press Start. 7. When done, aubergine will be tender. 8. Garnish with fresh basil to serve.

Chapter 4 Beef, Pork, and Lamb

Bacon and Cheese Stuffed Pork Chops

Prep time: 10 minutes | Cook time: 12 minutes | Serves 4

- 15 g plain pork scratchings, finely crushed
- 120 g shredded sharp Cheddar cheese
- 4 slices cooked bacon, crumbled
- 4 (110 g) boneless pork chops
- ½ teaspoon salt
- ¼ teaspoon ground black pepper

1. In a small bowl, mix pork scratchings, Cheddar, and bacon. 2. Make a 3-inch slit in the side of each pork chop and stuff with ¼ pork rind mixture. Sprinkle each side of pork chops with salt and pepper. 3. Place pork chops into ungreased air fryer basket, stuffed side up. In zone 1, select the AIR FRY button, adjust temperature to 200ºC, set time to 12 minutes. In zone 2, select Match Cook and press Start. Pork chops will be browned and have an internal temperature of at least 64ºC when done. Serve warm.

Cajun Bacon Pork Loin Fillet

Prep time: 30 minutes | Cook time: 20 minutes | Serves 6

- 680 g pork loin fillet or pork tenderloin
- 3 tablespoons olive oil
- 2 tablespoons Cajun spice mix
- Salt, to taste
- 6 slices bacon
- Olive oil spray

1. Cut the pork in half so that it will fit in the air fryer basket. 2. Place both pieces of meat in a resealable plastic bag. Add the oil, Cajun seasoning, and salt to taste, if using. Seal the bag and massage to coat all of the meat with the oil and seasonings. Marinate in the refrigerator for at least 1 hour or up to 24 hours. 3. Remove the pork from the bag and wrap 3 bacon slices around each piece. Spray the air fryer basket with olive oil spray. Place the meat in the air fryer. In zone 1, select the AIR FRY button, adjust temperature to 180ºC, set time to 15 minutes. In zone 2, select Match Cook and press Start. Increase the temperature to 200ºC for 5 minutes. Use a meat thermometer to ensure the meat has reached an internal temperature of 64ºC. 4. Let the meat rest for 10 minutes. Slice into 6 medallions and serve.

Chorizo and Beef Burger

Prep time: 10 minutes | Cook time: 15 minutes | Serves 4

- 340 g 80/20 beef mince
- 110 g Mexican-style chorizo crumb
- 60 g chopped onion
- 5 slices pickled jalapeños, chopped
- 2 teaspoons chilli powder
- 1 teaspoon minced garlic
- ¼ teaspoon cumin

1. In a large bowl, mix all ingredients. Divide the mixture into four sections and form them into burger patties. 2. Place burger patties into the air fryer basket. 3. In zone 1, select the AIR FRY button, adjust temperature to 190ºC, set time to 15 minutes. In zone 2, select Match Cook and press Start. . 4. Flip the patties halfway through the cooking time. Serve warm.

Pork and Pinto Bean Gorditas

Prep timePork and Pinto Bean Gorditas

- 450 g lean pork mince
- 2 tablespoons chilli powder
- 2 tablespoons ground cumin
- 1 teaspoon dried oregano
- 2 teaspoons paprika
- 1 teaspoon garlic powder
- 120 ml water
- 1 (425 g) tin pinto beans, drained and rinsed
- 120 ml salsa
- Salt and freshly ground black pepper, to taste
- 475 g grated Cheddar cheese
- 5 (12-inch) flour maize wraps
- 4 (8-inch) crispy maize taco shells
- 1 kg shredded lettuce
- 1 tomato, diced
- 80 g sliced black olives
- Sour cream, for serving
- Tomato salsa, for serving
- Cooking spray

1. Preheat the air fryer to 200ºC. Spritz the air fryer basket with cooking spray. 2. In zone 1, select the AIR FRY button, adjust temperature to 200ºC, set time to 10 minutes. In zone 2, select Match Cook and press Start, stirring a few times to gently break up the meat. Combine the chilli powder, cumin, oregano, paprika, garlic powder and water in a small bowl. Stir the spice mixture into the browned pork. Stir in the beans and salsa and air fry for an additional minute. Transfer the pork mixture to a bowl. Season with salt and freshly ground black pepper. 3. Sprinkle 120 ml of the grated cheese in the center of the flour maize wraps, leaving a 2-inch border around the edge free of cheese and filling. Divide the pork mixture among the four maize wraps, placing it on top of the cheese. Put a taco shell on top of the pork and top with shredded lettuce, diced tomatoes, and black olives. Cut the remaining flour maize wrap into 4 quarters. These quarters of maize wrap will serve as the bottom of the gordita. Put one quarter maize wrap on top of each gordita and fold the edges of the bottom flour maize wrap up over the sides, enclosing the filling. While holding the seams down, brush the bottom of the gordita with olive oil and place the seam side down on the countertop while you finish the remaining three gorditas. 4. Adjust the temperature to 190ºC. 5. Air fry one gordita at a time. Transfer the gordita carefully to the air fryer basket, seam side down. Brush or spray the top maize wrap with oil and air fry for 5 minutes. Carefully turn the gordita over and air fry for an additional 4 to 5 minutes until both sides are browned. When finished air frying all four gorditas, layer them back into the air fryer for an additional minute to make sure they are all warm before serving with sour cream and salsa.

Chapter 4 Beef, Pork, and Lamb

Steak with Pepper

Prep time: 30 minutes | Cook time: 20 to 23 minutes | Serves 6

- 60 ml avocado oil
- 60 g freshly squeezed lime juice
- 2 teaspoons minced garlic
- 1 tablespoon chilli powder
- ½ teaspoon ground cumin
- Sea salt and freshly ground black pepper, to taste
- 450 g top rump steak or bavette or skirt steak, thinly sliced against the grain
- 1 red pepper, cored, seeded, and cut into ½-inch slices
- 1 green pepper, cored, seeded, and cut into ½-inch slices
- 1 large onion, sliced

1. In a small bowl or blender, combine the avocado oil, lime juice, garlic, chilli powder, cumin, and salt and pepper to taste. 2. Place the sliced steak in a zip-top bag or shallow dish. Place the peppers and onion in a separate zip-top bag or dish. Pour half the marinade over the steak and the other half over the vegetables. Seal both bags and let the steak and vegetables marinate in the refrigerator for at least 1 hour or up to 4 hours. 3. Line the air fryer basket with an air fryer liner or aluminium foil. Remove the vegetables from their bag or dish and shake off any excess marinade. Set the air fryer to 200ºC. Place the vegetables in the air fryer basket and cook for 13 minutes. 4. Remove the steak from its bag or dish and shake off any excess marinade. Place the steak on top of the vegetables in the air fryer. In zone 1, select the AIR FRY button, and set time to 7 to 10 minutes or until an instant-read thermometer reads 49ºC for medium-rare (or cook to your desired doneness). . In zone 2, select Match Cook and press Start. 5. Serve with desired fixings, such as keto maize wraps, lettuce, sour cream, avocado slices, shredded Cheddar cheese, and coriander.

Mojito Lamb Chops

Prep time: 30 minutes | Cook time: 5 minutes | Serves 2

Marinade:

- 2 teaspoons grated lime zest
- 120 ml lime juice
- 60 ml avocado oil
- 60 g chopped fresh mint leaves
- 4 cloves garlic, roughly chopped
- 2 teaspoons fine sea salt
- ½ teaspoon ground black pepper
- 4 (1-inch-thick) lamb chops
- Sprigs of fresh mint, for garnish (optional)
- Lime slices, for serving (optional)

1. Make the marinade: Place all the ingredients for the marinade in a food processor or blender and purée until mostly smooth with a few small chunks. Transfer half of the marinade to a shallow dish and set the other half aside for serving. Add the lamb to the shallow dish, cover, and place in the refrigerator to marinate for at least 2 hours or overnight. 2. Spray the air fryer basket with avocado oil. Preheat the air fryer to 200ºC. 3. Remove the chops from the marinade and place them in the air fryer basket. In zone 1, select the AIR FRY button, and set time to 5 minutes, or until the internal temperature reaches 64ºC for medium doneness. In zone 2, select Match Cook and press Start. 4. Allow the chops to rest for 10 minutes before serving with the rest of the marinade as a sauce. Garnish with fresh mint leaves and serve with lime slices, if desired. Best served fresh.

Italian Banger Links

Prep time: 10 minutes | Cook time: 24 minutes | Serves 4

- 1 pepper (any color), sliced
- 1 medium onion, sliced
- 1 tablespoon avocado oil
- 1 teaspoon Italian seasoning
- Sea salt and freshly ground black pepper, to taste
- 450 g Italian-seasoned banger links

1. Place the pepper and onion in a medium bowl, and toss with the avocado oil, Italian seasoning, and salt and pepper to taste. 2. Set the air fryer to 200°C. Put the vegetables in the air fryer basket and cook for 12 minutes. 3. Push the vegetables to the side of the basket and arrange the banger links in the bottom of the basket in a single layer. Spoon the vegetables over the bangers. In zone 1, select the AIR FRY button, and set time to 12 minutes, until an instant-read thermometer inserted into the banger reads 72°C. In zone 2, select Match Cook and press Start, tossing halfway through

Nigerian Peanut-Crusted Bavette Steak

Prep time: 30 minutes | Cook time: 8 minutes | Serves 4

Suya Spice Mix:

- 60 g dry-roasted peanuts
- 1 teaspoon cumin seeds
- 1 teaspoon garlic powder
- 1 teaspoon smoked paprika
- ½ teaspoon ground ginger
- 1 teaspoon coarse or flaky salt
- ½ teaspoon cayenne pepper

Steak:

- 450 g bavette or skirt steak
- 2 tablespoons vegetable oil

1. For the spice mix: In a clean coffee grinder or spice mill, combine the peanuts and cumin seeds. Process until you get a coarse powder. (Do not overprocess or you will wind up with peanut butter! Alternatively, you tin grind the cumin with 80 g ready-made peanut powder instead of the peanuts.) 2. Pour the peanut mixture into a small bowl, add the garlic powder, paprika, ginger, salt, and cayenne, and stir to combine. This recipe makes about 120 ml suya spice mix. Store leftovers in an airtight container in a cool, dry place for up to 1 month. 3. For the steak: Cut the steak into ½-inch-thick slices, cutting against the grain and at a slight angle. Place the beef strips in a resealable plastic bag and add the oil and 2½ to 3 tablespoons of the spice mixture. Seal the bag and massage to coat all of the meat with the oil and spice mixture. Marinate at room temperature for 30 minutes or in the refrigerator for up to 24 hours. 4. Place the beef strips in the air fryer basket. In zone 1, select the AIR FRY button, adjust temperature to 200°C, set time to 8 minutes. In zone 2, select Match Cook and press Start, turning the strips halfway through the cooking time. 5. Transfer the meat to a serving platter. Sprinkle with additional spice mix, if desired.

Spicy Lamb Sirloin Chops

Prep time: 30 minutes | Cook time: 15 minutes | Serves 4

- ½ brown onion, coarsely chopped
- 4 coin-size slices peeled fresh ginger
- 5 garlic cloves
- 1 teaspoon garam masala
- 1 teaspoon ground fennel
- 1 teaspoon ground cinnamon
- 1 teaspoon ground turmeric
- ½ to 1 teaspoon cayenne pepper
- ½ teaspoon ground cardamom
- 1 teaspoon coarse or flaky salt
- 450 g lamb sirloin chops

1. In a blender, combine the onion, ginger, garlic, garam masala, fennel, cinnamon, turmeric, cayenne, cardamom, and salt. Pulse until the onion is finely minced and the mixture forms a thick paste, 3 to 4 minutes. 2. Place the lamb chops in a large bowl. Slash the meat and fat with a sharp knife several times to allow the marinade to penetrate better. Add the spice paste to the bowl and toss the lamb to coat. Marinate at room temperature for 30 minutes or cover and refrigerate for up to 24 hours. 3. Place the lamb chops in a single layer in the air fryer basket. In zone 1, select the AIR FRY button, adjust temperature to 160ºC, set time to 15 minutes. In zone 2, select Match Cook and press Start, turning the chops halfway through the cooking time. Use a meat thermometer to ensure the lamb has reached an internal temperature of 64ºC (medium-rare).

Almond and Caraway Crust Steak

Prep time: 16 minutes | Cook time: 10 minutes | Serves 4

- 40 g almond flour
- 2 eggs
- 2 teaspoons caraway seeds
- 4 beef steaks
- 2 teaspoons garlic powder
- 1 tablespoon melted butter
- Fine sea salt and cayenne pepper, to taste

1. Generously coat steaks with garlic powder, caraway seeds, salt, and cayenne pepper. 2. In a mixing dish, thoroughly combine melted butter with seasoned crumbs. In another bowl, beat the eggs until they're well whisked. 3. First, coat steaks with the beaten egg; then, coat beef steaks with the buttered crumb mixture. In zone 1, select the AIR FRY button, adjust temperature to 180ºC, set time to 10 minutes. In zone 2, select Match Cook and press Start. Bon appétit!

Sirloin Steak with Honey-Mustard Butter

Prep time: 5 minutes | Cook time: 14 minutes | Serves 4

- 900 g beef sirloin steak
- 1 teaspoon cayenne pepper
- 1 tablespoon honey
- 1 tablespoon Dijon mustard
- ½ stick butter, softened
- Sea salt and freshly ground black pepper, to taste
- Cooking spray

1. Preheat the air fryer to 200ºC and spritz with cooking spray. 2. Sprinkle the steak with cayenne pepper, salt, and black pepper on a clean work surface. 3. Arrange the steak in the preheated air fryer and spritz with cooking spray. 4. In zone 1, select the AIR FRY button, and set time to 14 minutes or until browned and reach your desired doneness.. In zone 2, select Match Cook and press Start. Flip the steak halfway through. 5. Meanwhile, combine the honey, mustard, and butter in a small bowl. Stir to mix well. 6. Transfer the air fried steak onto a plate and baste with the honey-mustard butter before serving.

Lamb and Cucumber Burgers

Prep time: 8 minutes | Cook time: 15 to 18 minutes | Serves 4

- 1 teaspoon ground ginger
- ½ teaspoon ground coriander
- ¼ teaspoon freshly ground white pepper
- ½ teaspoon ground cinnamon
- ½ teaspoon dried oregano
- ¼ teaspoon ground allspice
- ¼ teaspoon ground turmeric
- 120 ml low-fat plain Greek yoghurt
- 450 g lamb mince
- 1 teaspoon garlic paste
- ¼ teaspoon salt
- ¼ teaspoon freshly ground black pepper
- Cooking oil spray
- 4 hamburger buns
- ½ cucumber, thinly sliced

1. In a small bowl, stir together the ginger, coriander, white pepper, cinnamon, oregano, allspice, and turmeric. 2. Put the yoghurt in a small bowl and add half the spice mixture. Mix well and refrigerate. 3. Insert the crisper plate into the basket and the basket into the unit. Preheat the unit by selecting AIR FRY, setting the temperature to 180ºC, and setting the time to 3 minutes. Select START/STOP to begin. 4. In a large bowl, combine the lamb, garlic paste, remaining spice mix, salt, and pepper. Gently but thoroughly mix the ingredients with your hands. Form the meat into 4 patties. 5. Once the unit is preheated, spray the crisper plate with cooking oil, and place the patties into the basket. 6. In zone 1, select the AIR FRY button, adjust temperature to 180ºC, set time to 18 minutes. In zone 2, select Match Cook and press Start. 7. After 15 minutes, check the burgers. If a food thermometer inserted into the burgers registers 72ºC, the burgers are done. If not, resume cooking. 8. When the cooking is complete, assemble the burgers on the buns with cucumber slices and a dollop of the yoghurt dip.

Tuscan Air Fried Veal Loin

Prep time: 1 hour 10 minutes | Cook time: 12 minutes | Makes 3 veal chops

- 1½ teaspoons crushed fennel seeds
- 1 tablespoon minced fresh rosemary leaves
- 1 tablespoon minced garlic
- 1½ teaspoons lemon zest
- 1½ teaspoons salt
- ½ teaspoon red pepper flakes
- 2 tablespoons olive oil
- 3 (280 g) bone-in veal loin, about ½ inch thick

1. Combine all the ingredients, except for the veal loin, in a large bowl. Stir to mix well. 2. Dunk the loin in the mixture and press to submerge. Wrap the bowl in plastic and refrigerate for at least an hour to marinate. 3. Preheat the air fryer to 200ºC. 4. Arrange the veal loin in the preheated air fryer. In zone 1, select the AIR FRY button, and set time to 12 minutes for medium-rare, or until it reaches your desired doneness. In zone 2, select Match Cook and press Start. 5. Serve immediately.

Kheema Burgers

Prep time: 15 minutes | Cook time: 12 minutes | Serves 4

- 450 g 85% lean beef mince or lamb mince
- 2 large eggs, lightly beaten
- 1 medium brown onion, diced
- 60 g chopped fresh coriander
- 1 tablespoon minced fresh ginger
- 3 cloves garlic, minced
- 235 g grated cucumber
- 120 ml sour cream
- 4 lettuce leaves, hamburger buns, or naan breads

Burgers:
- 2 teaspoons garam masala
- 1 teaspoon ground turmeric
- ½ teaspoon ground cinnamon
- ⅛ teaspoon ground cardamom
- 1 teaspoon coarse or flaky salt
- 1 teaspoon cayenne pepper

Raita Sauce:
- ¼ teaspoon coarse or flaky salt
- ¼ teaspoon black pepper

For Serving:

1. For the burgers: In a large bowl, combine the beef mince, eggs, onion, coriander, ginger, garlic, garam masala, turmeric, cinnamon, cardamom, salt, and cayenne. Gently mix until ingredients are thoroughly combined. 2. Divide the meat into four portions and form into round patties. Make a slight depression in the middle of each patty with your thumb to prevent them from puffing up into a dome shape while cooking. 3. Place the patties in the air fryer basket. In zone 1, select the AIR FRY button, adjust temperature to 180ºC, set time to 12 minutes. In zone 2, select Match Cook and press Start. Use a meat thermometer to ensure the burgers have reached an internal temperature of 72ºC (for medium). 4. Meanwhile, for the sauce: In a small bowl, combine the cucumber, sour cream, salt, and pepper. 5. To serve: Place the burgers on the lettuce, buns, or naan and top with the sauce.

Steak, Broccoli, and Mushroom Rice Bowls

Prep time: 10 minutes | Cook time: 15 to 18 minutes | Serves 4

- 2 tablespoons cornflour
- 120 ml low-sodium beef stock
- 1 teaspoon reduced-salt soy sauce
- 340 g rump steak, cut into 1-inch cubes
- 120 g broccoli florets
- 1 onion, chopped
- 235 g sliced white or chestnut mushrooms
- 1 tablespoon grated peeled fresh ginger
- Cooked brown rice (optional), for serving

1. In a medium bowl, stir together the cornflour, beef stock, and soy sauce until the cornflour is completely dissolved. 2. Add the beef cubes and toss to coat. Let stand for 5 minutes at room temperature. 3. Insert the crisper plate into the basket and the basket into the unit. Preheat the unit by selecting AIR FRY, setting the temperature to 200ºC, and setting the time to 3 minutes. Select START/STOP to begin. 4. Once the unit is preheated, use a slotted spoon to transfer the beef from the stock mixture into a medium metal bowl that fits into the basket. Reserve the stock. Add the broccoli, onion, mushrooms, and ginger to the beef. Place the bowl into the basket. 5. In zone 1, select the AIR FRY button, adjust temperature to 200ºC, set time to 18 minutes. In zone 2, select Match Cook and press Start. 6. After about 12 minutes, check the beef and broccoli. If a food thermometer inserted into the beef registers at least 64ºC and the vegetables are tender, add the reserved stock and resume cooking for about 3 minutes until the sauce boils. If not, resume cooking for about 3 minutes before adding the reservedstock. 7. When the cooking is complete, serve immediately over hot cooked brown rice, if desired.

Pork Loin Roast

Prep time: 30 minutes | Cook time: 55 minutes | Serves 6

- 680 g boneless pork loin joint, washed
- 1 teaspoon mustard seeds
- 1 teaspoon garlic powder
- 1 teaspoon porcini powder
- 1 teaspoon onion granules
- ¾ teaspoon sea salt flakes
- 1 teaspoon red pepper flakes, crushed
- 2 dried sprigs thyme, crushed
- 2 tablespoons lime juice

1. Firstly, score the meat using a small knife; make sure to not cut too deep. 2. In a small-sized mixing dish, combine all seasonings in the order listed above; mix to combine well. 3. Massage the spice mix into the pork meat to evenly distribute. Drizzle with lemon juice. 4. In zone 1, select the ROAST button, adjust temperature to 180ºC, set time to 25 to 30 minutes. In zone 2, select Match Cook and press Start. Pause the machine, check for doneness and cook for 25 minutes more.

Deconstructed Chicago Dogs

Prep time: 10 minutes | Cook time: 7 minutes | Serves 4

- 4 hot dogs
- 2 large dill pickles
- 60 g diced onions
- 1 tomato, cut into ½-inch dice
- 4 pickled or brined jalapeno peppers, diced
- For Garnish (Optional):
- Wholegrain or Dijon mustard
- Celery salt
- Poppy seeds

1. Spray the air fryer basket with avocado oil. Preheat the air fryer to 200ºC. 2. Place the hot dogs in the air fryer basket. In zone 1, select the AIR FRY button, and set time to 5 to 7 minutes until hot and slightly crispy. In zone 2, select Match Cook and press Start. 3. While the hot dogs cook, quarter one of the dill pickles lengthwise, so that you have 4 gherkin spears. Finely dice the other pickle. 4. When the hot dogs are done, transfer them to a serving platter and arrange them in a row, alternating with the gherkin spears. Top with the diced pickles, onions, tomato, and jalapeno peppers. Drizzle mustard on top and garnish with celery salt and poppy seeds, if desired. 5. Best served fresh. Store leftover hot dogs in an airtight container in the refrigerator for up to 3 days. Reheat in a preheated 200ºC air fryer for 2 minutes, or until warmed through.

Panko Crusted Calf's Liver Strips

Prep time: 15 minutes | Cook time: 23 to 25 minutes | Serves 4

- 450 g sliced calf's liver, cut into ½-inch wide strips
- 2 eggs
- 2 tablespoons milk
- 60 g whole wheat flour
- 240 g panko breadcrumbs
- Salt and ground black pepper, to taste
- Cooking spray

1. Preheat the air fryer to 200ºC and spritz with cooking spray. 2. Rub the calf's liver strips with salt and ground black pepper on a clean work surface. 3. Whisk the eggs with milk in a large bowl. Pour the flour in a shallow dish. Pour the panko on a separate shallow dish. 4. Dunk the liver strips in the flour, then in the egg mixture. Shake the excess off and roll the strips over the panko to coat well. 5. Arrange the liver strips in a single layer in the preheated air fryer and spritz with cooking spray. 6. In zone 1, select the AIR FRY button, and set time to 5 minutes or until browned. In zone 2, select Match Cook and press Start. Flip the strips halfway through. 7. Serve immediately.

Sichuan Cumin Lamb

Prep time: 30 minutes | Cook time: 10 minutes | Serves 4

Lamb:

- 2 tablespoons cumin seeds
- 1 teaspoon Sichuan peppercorns, or ½ teaspoon cayenne pepper
- 450 g lamb (preferably shoulder), cut into ½ by 2-inch pieces
- 2 tablespoons vegetable oil
- 1 tablespoon light soy sauce
- 2 spring onions, chopped
- 1 tablespoon minced garlic
- 2 fresh red chillies, chopped
- 1 teaspoon coarse or flaky salt
- ¼ teaspoon sugar

For Serving:

- Large handful of chopped fresh coriander

1. For the lamb: In a dry frying pan, toast the cumin seeds and Sichuan peppercorns (if using) over medium heat, stirring frequently, until fragrant, 1 to 2 minutes. Remove from the heat and let cool. Use a mortar and pestle to coarsely grind the toasted spices. 2. Use a fork to pierce the lamb pieces to allow the marinade to penetrate better. In a large bowl or resealable plastic bag, combine the toasted spices, vegetable oil, soy sauce, garlic, chillies, salt, and sugar. Add the lamb to the bag. Seal and massage to coat. Marinate at room temperature for 30 minutes. 3. Place the lamb in a single layer in the air fryer basket. In zone 1, select the AIR FRY button, adjust temperature to 180ºC, set time to 10 minutes. In zone 2, select Match Cook and press Start. Use a meat thermometer to ensure the lamb has reached an internal temperature of 64ºC (medium-rare). 4. Transfer the lamb to a serving bowl. Stir in the spring onionspring onions and coriander and serve.

Cheese Pork Chops

Prep time: 15 minutes | Cook time: 9 to 14 minutes | Serves 4

- 2 large eggs
- 120 g finely grated Parmesan cheese
- 60 g finely ground blanched almond flour or finely crushed pork scratchings
- 1 teaspoon paprika
- ½ teaspoon dried oregano
- ½ teaspoon garlic powder
- Salt and freshly ground black pepper, to taste
- 570 g (1-inch-thick) boneless pork chops
- Avocado oil spray

1. Beat the eggs in a shallow bowl. In a separate bowl, combine the Parmesan cheese, almond flour, paprika, oregano, garlic powder, and salt and pepper to taste. 2. Dip the pork chops into the eggs, then coat them with the Parmesan mixture, gently pressing the coating onto the meat. Spray the breaded pork chops with oil. 3. Place the pork chops in the air fryer basket in a single layer. In zone 1, select the AIR FRY button, adjust temperature to 100ºC, set time to 6 minutes. In zone 2, select Match Cook and press Start. Flip the chops and spray them with more oil. Cook for another 3 to 8 minutes, until an instant-read thermometer reads 64ºC. 4. Allow the pork chops to rest for at least 5 minutes, then serve.

Chapter 5   Fish and Seafood

Salmon Fritters with Courgette

Prep time: 15 minutes | Cook time: 12 minutes | Serves 4

- 2 tablespoons almond flour
- 1 courgette, grated
- 1 egg, beaten
- 170 g salmon fillet, diced
- 1 teaspoon avocado oil
- ½ teaspoon ground black pepper

1. Mix almond flour with courgette, egg, salmon, and ground black pepper. 2. Then make the fritters from the salmon mixture. 3. Sprinkle the air fryer basket with avocado oil and put the fritters inside. 4. In zone 1, select the AIR FRY button, adjust temperature to 190ºC, set time to 6 minutes per side. In zone 2, select Match Cook and press Start.

Cod with Avocado

Prep time: 30 minutes | Cook time: 10 minutes | Serves 2

- 90 g shredded cabbage
- 60 ml full-fat sour cream
- 2 tablespoons full-fat mayonnaise
- 20 g chopped pickled jalapeños
- 2 (85 g) cod fillets
- 1 teaspoon chilli powder
- 1 teaspoon cumin
- ½ teaspoon paprika
- ¼ teaspoon garlic powder
- 1 medium avocado, peeled, pitted, and sliced
- ½ medium lime

1. In a large bowl, place cabbage, sour cream, mayonnaise, and jalapeños. Mix until fully coated. Let sit for 20 minutes in the refrigerator. 2. Sprinkle cod fillets with chilli powder, cumin, paprika, and garlic powder. Place each fillet into the air fryer basket. 3. In zone 1, select the AIR FRY button, adjust temperature to 190ºC, set time to 10 minutes. In zone 2, select Match Cook and press Start. 4. Flip the fillets halfway through the cooking time. When fully cooked, fish should have an internal temperature of at least 64ºC. 5. To serve, divide slaw mixture into two serving bowls, break cod fillets into pieces and spread over the bowls, and top with avocado. Squeeze lime juice over each bowl. Serve immediately.

Sweet Tilapia Fillets

Prep time: 5 minutes | Cook time: 14 minutes | Serves 4

- 2 tablespoons granulated sweetener
- 1 tablespoon apple cider vinegar
- 4 tilapia fillets, boneless
- 1 teaspoon olive oil

1. Mix apple cider vinegar with olive oil and sweetener. 2. Then rub the tilapia fillets with the sweet mixture and put in the air fryer basket in one layer. In zone 1, select the AIR FRY button, adjust temperature to 180ºC, set time to 7 minutes per side. In zone 2, select Match Cook and press Start.

Fish Croquettes with Lemon-Dill Aioli

Prep time: 15 minutes | Cook time: 10 minutes | Serves 4

Croquettes:

- 3 large eggs, divided
- 340 g raw cod fillet, flaked apart with two forks
- 60 ml skimmed milk
- 190 g boxed instant mashed potatoes
- 2 teaspoons olive oil
- 8 g chopped fresh dill
- 1 shallot, minced
- 1 large garlic clove, minced
- 60 g breadcrumbs plus 2 tablespoons, divided
- 1 teaspoon fresh lemon juice
- 1 teaspoon kosher or coarse sea salt
- ½ teaspoon dried thyme
- ¼ teaspoon freshly ground black pepper
- Cooking spray

Lemon-Dill Aioli:

- 5 tablespoons mayonnaise
- Juice of ½ lemon
- 1 tablespoon chopped fresh dill

1. For the croquettes: In a medium bowl, lightly beat 2 of the eggs. Add the fish, milk, instant mashed potatoes, olive oil, dill, shallot, and garlic, 2 tablespoons of the bread crumbs, lemon juice, salt, thyme, and pepper. Mix to thoroughly combine. Place in the refrigerator for 30 minutes. 2. For the lemon-dill aioli: In a small bowl, combine the mayonnaise, lemon juice, and dill. Set aside. 3. Measure out about 3½ tablespoons of the fish mixture and gently roll in your hands to form a log about 3 inches long. Repeat to make a total of 12 logs. 4. Beat the remaining egg in a small bowl. Place the remaining ¾ cup bread crumbs in a separate bowl. Dip the croquettes in the egg, then coat in the bread crumbs, gently pressing to adhere. Place on a work surface and spray both sides with cooking spray. 5. Preheat the air fryer to 180ºC. 6. Arrange a single layer of the croquettes in the air fryer basket. In zone 1, select the AIR FRY button, and set time to 10 minutes. In zone 2, select Match Cook and press Start, flipping halfway, until golden. 7. Serve with the aioli for dipping.

Snapper Scampi

Prep time: 5 minutes | Cook time: 8 to 10 minutes | Serves 4

- 4 skinless snapper or arctic char fillets, 170 g each
- 1 tablespoon olive oil
- 3 tablespoons lemon juice, divided
- ½ teaspoon dried basil
- Pinch salt
- Freshly ground black pepper, to taste
- 2 tablespoons butter
- 2 cloves garlic, minced

1. Rub the fish fillets with olive oil and 1 tablespoon of the lemon juice. Sprinkle with the basil, salt, and pepper, and place in the air fryer basket. 2. In zone 1, select the AIR FRY button, adjust temperature to 190ºC, set time to 7 to 8 minutes or until the fish just flakes when tested with a fork. In zone 2, select Match Cook and press Start. Remove the fish from the basket and put on a serving plate. Cover to keep warm. 3. In a baking pan, combine the butter, remaining 2 tablespoons lemon juice, and garlic. Bake in the air fryer for 1 to 2 minutes or until the garlic is sizzling. Pour this mixture over the fish and serve.

Crab Cake Sandwich

Prep time: 15 minutes | Cook time: 10 minutes | Serves 4

- 60 g panko bread crumbs
- 1 large egg, beaten
- 1 large egg white
- 1 tablespoon mayonnaise
- 1 teaspoon Dijon mustard
- 5 g minced fresh parsley
- 1 tablespoon fresh lemon juice

- 60 g mayonnaise
- 1 tablespoon minced dill pickle

- 4 round lettuce leaves

Crab Cakes:
- ½ teaspoon Old Bay seasoning
- ⅛ teaspoon sweet paprika
- ⅛ teaspoon kosher or coarse sea salt
- Freshly ground black pepper, to taste
- 280 g lump crab meat
- Cooking spray

Cajun Mayo:
- 1 teaspoon fresh lemon juice
- ¾ teaspoon Cajun seasoning

For Serving:
- 4 whole wheat potato buns or gluten-free buns

1. For the crab cakes: In a large bowl, combine the panko, whole egg, egg white, mayonnaise, mustard, parsley, lemon juice, Old Bay, paprika, salt, and pepper to taste and mix well. Fold in the crab meat, being careful not to over mix. Gently shape into 4 round patties, ¾ inch thick. Spray both sides with oil. 2. Preheat the air fryer to 190ºC. 3. Place the crab cakes in the air fryer basket. In zone 1, select the AIR FRY button, and set time to 10 minutes. In zone 2, select Match Cook and press Start, flipping halfway, until the edges are golden. 4. Meanwhile, for the Cajun mayo: In a small bowl, combine the mayonnaise, pickle, lemon juice, and Cajun seasoning. 5. To serve: Place a lettuce leaf on each bun bottom and top with a crab cake and a generous tablespoon of Cajun mayonnaise. Add the bun top and serve.

Garlic Butter Prawns Scampi

Prep time: 5 minutes | Cook time: 8 minutes | Serves 4

- 60 g unsalted butter
- 2 tablespoons fish stock or chicken broth
- 2 cloves garlic, minced
- 2 tablespoons chopped fresh basil leaves

Prawns:

- 455 g large prawns, peeled and deveined, tails removed

Sauce:

- 1 tablespoon lemon juice
- 1 tablespoon chopped fresh parsley, plus more for garnish
- 1 teaspoon red pepper flakes

- Fresh basil sprigs, for garnish

1. Preheat the air fryer to 180ºC. 2. Put all the ingredients for the sauce in a baking pan and stir to incorporate. 3. Transfer the baking pan to the air fryer and air fry for 3 minutes, or until the sauce is heated through. 4. Once done, add the prawns to the baking pan, flipping to coat in the sauce. 5. Return to the air fryer and cook for another 5 minutes, or until the prawns are pink and opaque. Stir the prawns twice during cooking. 6. Serve garnished with the parsley and basil sprigs.

Lemon-Pepper Trout

Prep time: 5 minutes | Cook time: 15 minutes | Serves 4

- 4 trout fillets
- 2 tablespoons olive oil
- ½ teaspoon salt
- 1 teaspoon black pepper
- 2 garlic cloves, sliced
- 1 lemon, sliced, plus additional wedges for serving

1. Preheat the air fryer to 190ºC. 2. Brush each fillet with olive oil on both sides and season with salt and pepper. Place the fillets in an even layer in the air fryer basket. 3. Place the sliced garlic over the tops of the trout fillets, then top the garlic with lemon slices. In zone 1, select the ROAST button, and set time to 12 to 15 minutes or until it has reached an internal temperature of 64ºC. In zone 2, select Match Cook and press Start. 4. Serve with fresh lemon wedges.

Garlic Lemon Scallops

Prep time: 5 minutes | Cook time: 10 minutes | Serves 4

- 4 tablespoons salted butter, melted
- 4 teaspoons peeled and finely minced garlic
- ½ small lemon, zested and juiced
- 8 sea scallops, 30 g each, cleaned and patted dry
- ¼ teaspoon salt
- ¼ teaspoon ground black pepper

1. In a small bowl, mix butter, garlic, lemon zest, and lemon juice. Place scallops in an ungreased round nonstick baking dish. Pour butter mixture over scallops, then sprinkle with salt and pepper. 2. Place dish into air fryer basket. In zone 1, select the BAKE button, adjust temperature to 180ºC, set time to 10 minutes. In zone 2, select Match Cook and press Start. Scallops will be opaque and firm, and have an internal temperature of 56ºC when done. Serve warm.

Roasted Salmon Fillets

Prep time: 5 minutes | Cook time: 10 minutes | Serves 2

- 2 (230 g) skin-on salmon fillets, 1½ inches thick
- 1 teaspoon vegetable oil
- Salt and pepper, to taste
- Vegetable oil spray

1. Preheat the air fryer to 200ºC. 2. Make foil sling for air fryer basket by folding 1 long sheet of aluminium foil so it is 4 inches wide. Lay sheet of foil widthwise across basket, pressing foil into and up sides of basket. Fold excess foil as needed so that edges of foil are flush with top of basket. Lightly spray foil and basket with vegetable oil spray. 3. Pat salmon dry with paper towels, rub with oil, and season with salt and pepper. Arrange fillets skin side down on sling in prepared basket, spaced evenly apart. Air fry salmon until center is still translucent when checked with the tip of a paring knife and registers 52ºC (for medium-rare), 10 to 14 minutes, using sling to rotate fillets halfway through cooking. 4. Using the sling, carefully remove salmon from air fryer. Slide fish spatula along underside of fillets and transfer to individual serving plates, leaving skin behind. Serve.

Browned Prawns Patties

Prep time: 15 minutes | Cook time: 10 to 12 minutes | Serves 4

- 230 g raw prawns, peeled, deveined and chopped finely
- 500 g cooked sushi rice
- 35 g chopped red pepper
- 35 g chopped celery
- 35 g chopped spring onion
- 2 teaspoons Worcestershire sauce
- ½ teaspoon salt
- ½ teaspoon garlic powder
- ½ teaspoon Old Bay seasoning
- 75 g plain bread crumbs
- Cooking spray

1. Preheat the air fryer to 200°C. 2. Put all the ingredients except the bread crumbs and oil in a large bowl and stir to incorporate. 3. Scoop out the prawn mixture and shape into 8 equal-sized patties with your hands, no more than ½-inch thick. Roll the patties in the bread crumbs on a plate and spray both sides with cooking spray. 4. Place the patties in the air fryer basket. 5. In zone 1, select the AIR FRY button, and set time to 10 to 12 minutes. In zone 2, select Match Cook and press Start, flipping the patties halfway through, or until the outside is crispy brown. 6. Divide the patties among four plates and serve warm.

Almond-Crusted Fish

Prep time: 15 minutes | Cook time: 10 minutes | Serves 4

- 4 firm white fish fillets, 110g each
- 25 g breadcrumbs
- 20 g slivered almonds, crushed
- 2 tablespoons lemon juice
- ⅛ teaspoon cayenne
- Salt and pepper, to taste
- 470 g plain flour
- 1 egg, beaten with 1 tablespoon water
- Olive or vegetable oil for misting or cooking spray

1. Split fish fillets lengthwise down the center to create 8 pieces. 2. Mix breadcrumbs and almonds together and set aside. 3. Mix the lemon juice and cayenne together. Brush on all sides of fish. 4. Season fish to taste with salt and pepper. 5. Place the flour on a sheet of wax paper. 6. Roll fillets in flour, dip in egg wash, and roll in the crumb mixture. 7. Mist both sides of fish with oil or cooking spray. 8. Spray the air fryer basket and lay fillets inside. 9. In zone 1, select the ROAST button, adjust temperature to 200°C, set time to 5 minutes. In zone 2, select Match Cook and press Start. Turn fish over, and cook for an additional 5 minutes or until fish is done and flakes easily.

Blackened Red Snapper

Prep time: 13 minutes | Cook time: 8 to 10 minutes | Serves 4

- 1½ teaspoons black pepper
- ¼ teaspoon thyme
- ¼ teaspoon garlic powder
- ⅛ teaspoon cayenne pepper
- 1 teaspoon olive oil
- 4 red snapper fillet portions, skin on, 110 g each
- 4 thin slices lemon
- Cooking spray

1. Mix the spices and oil together to make a paste. Rub into both sides of the fish. 2. Spray the air fryer basket with nonstick cooking spray and lay snapper steaks in basket, skin-side down. 3. Place a lemon slice on each piece of fish. 4. In zone 1, select the ROAST button, adjust temperature to 200°C, set time to 8 to 10 minutes. In zone 2, select Match Cook and press Start. The fish will not flake when done, but it should be white through the center.

Black Cod with Grapes and Kale

Prep time: 10 minutes | Cook time: 15 minutes | Serves 2

- 2 fillets of black cod, 200 g each
- Salt and freshly ground black pepper, to taste
- Olive oil
- 150 g grapes, halved
- 1 small bulb fennel, sliced ¼-inch thick
- 65 g pecans
- 200 g shredded kale
- 2 teaspoons white balsamic vinegar or white wine vinegar
- 2 tablespoons extra-virgin olive oil

1. Preheat the air fryer to 200°C. 2. Season the cod fillets with salt and pepper and drizzle, brush or spray a little olive oil on top. Place the fish, presentation side up (skin side down), into the air fryer basket. Air fry for 10 minutes. 3. When the fish has finished cooking, remove the fillets to a side plate and loosely tent with foil to rest. 4. Toss the grapes, fennel and pecans in a bowl with a drizzle of olive oil and season with salt and pepper. Add the grapes, fennel and pecans to the air fryer basket. In zone 1, select the AIR FRY button, and set time to 5 minutes. In zone 2, select Match Cook and press Start, shaking the basket once during the cooking time. 5. Transfer the grapes, fennel and pecans to a bowl with the kale. Dress the kale with the balsamic vinegar and olive oil, season to taste with salt and pepper and serve alongside the cooked fish.

Chilli Lime Prawns

Prep time: 5 minutes | Cook time: 5 minutes | Serves 4

- 455 g medium prawns, peeled and deveined
- 1 tablespoon salted butter, melted
- 2 teaspoons chilli powder
- ¼ teaspoon garlic powder
- ¼ teaspoon salt
- ¼ teaspoon ground black pepper
- ½ small lime, zested and juiced, divided

1. In a medium bowl, toss prawns with butter, then sprinkle with chilli powder, garlic powder, salt, pepper, and lime zest. 2. Place prawns into ungreased air fryer basket. In zone 1, select the AIR FRY button, adjust temperature to 200ºC, set time to 5 minutes. In zone 2, select Match Cook and press Start. Prawns will be firm and form a "C" shape when done. 3. Transfer prawns to a large serving dish and drizzle with lime juice. Serve warm.

Oyster Po'Boy

Prep time: 20 minutes | Cook time: 5 minutes | Serves 4

- 55 g plain flour
- 20 g yellow cornmeal
- 1 tablespoon Cajun seasoning
- 1 teaspoon salt
- 2 large eggs, beaten
- 1 teaspoon hot sauce
- 455 g pre-shucked oysters
- 1 (12-inch) French baguette, quartered and sliced horizontally
- Tartar Sauce, as needed
- 150 g shredded lettuce, divided
- 2 tomatoes, cut into slices
- Cooking spray

1. In a shallow bowl, whisk the flour, cornmeal, Cajun seasoning, and salt until blended. In a second shallow bowl, whisk together the eggs and hot sauce. 2. One at a time, dip the oysters in the cornmeal mixture, the eggs, and again in the cornmeal, coating thoroughly. 3. Preheat the air fryer to 200ºC. Line the air fryer basket with baking paper. 4. Place the oysters on the baking paper and spritz with oil. 5. In zone 1, select the AIR FRY button, and set time to 2 minutes. In zone 2, select Match Cook and press Start. Shake the basket, spritz the oysters with oil, and air fry for 3 minutes more until lightly browned and crispy. 6. Spread each sandwich half with Tartar Sauce. Assemble the po'boys by layering each sandwich with fried oysters, ½ cup shredded lettuce, and 2 tomato slices. 7. Serve immediately.

Snapper with Shallot and Tomato

Prep time: 20 minutes | Cook time: 15 minutes | Serves 2

- 2 snapper fillets
- 1 shallot, peeled and sliced
- 2 garlic cloves, halved
- 1 pepper, sliced
- 1 small-sized serrano pepper, sliced
- 1 tomato, sliced
- 1 tablespoon olive oil
- ¼ teaspoon freshly ground black pepper
- ½ teaspoon paprika
- Sea salt, to taste
- 2 bay leaves

1. Place two baking paper sheets on a working surface. Place the fish in the center of one side of the baking paper. 2. Top with the shallot, garlic, peppers, and tomato. Drizzle olive oil over the fish and vegetables. Season with black pepper, paprika, and salt. Add the bay leaves. 3. Fold over the other half of the baking paper. Now, fold the paper around the edges tightly and create a half moon shape, sealing the fish inside. 4. In zone 1, select the AIR FRY button, adjust temperature to 200ºC, set time to 15 minutes. In zone 2, select Match Cook and press Start. Serve warm.

Tuna with Herbs

Prep time: 20 minutes | Cook time: 17 minutes | Serves 4

- 1 tablespoon butter, melted
- 1 medium-sized leek, thinly sliced
- 1 tablespoon chicken stock
- 1 tablespoon dry white wine
- 455 g tuna
- ½ teaspoon red pepper flakes, crushed
- Sea salt and ground black pepper, to taste
- ½ teaspoon dried rosemary
- ½ teaspoon dried basil
- ½ teaspoon dried thyme
- 2 small ripe tomatoes, puréed
- 120 g Parmesan cheese, grated

1. Melt ½ tablespoon of butter in a sauté pan over medium-high heat. Now, cook the leek and garlic until tender and aromatic. Add the stock and wine to deglaze the pan. 2. Preheat the air fryer to 190ºC. 3. Grease a casserole dish with the remaining ½ tablespoon of melted butter. Place the fish in the casserole dish. Add the seasonings. Top with the sautéed leek mixture. Add the tomato purée. In zone 1, select the AIR FRY button, and set time to 10 minutes. In zone 2, select Match Cook and press Start. Top with grated Parmesan cheese; cook an additional 7 minutes until the crumbs are golden. Bon appétit!

Blackened Fish

Prep time: 15 minutes | Cook time: 8 minutes | Serves 4

- 1 large egg, beaten
- Blackened seasoning, as needed
- 2 tablespoons light brown sugar
- 4 tilapia fillets, 110g each
- Cooking spray

1. In a shallow bowl, place the beaten egg. In a second shallow bowl, stir together the Blackened seasoning and the brown sugar. 2. One at a time, dip the fish fillets in the egg, then the brown sugar mixture, coating thoroughly. 3. Preheat the air fryer to 150°C. Line the air fryer basket with baking paper. 4. Place the coated fish on the baking paper and spritz with oil. 5. In zone 1, select the BAKE button, and set time to 4 minutes. In zone 2, select Match Cook and press Start. Flip the fish, spritz it with oil, and bake for 4 to 6 minutes more until the fish is white inside and flakes easily with a fork. 6. Serve immediately.

Classic Fish Fingers with Tartar Sauce

Prep time: 10 minutes | Cook time: 12 to 15 minutes | Serves 4

- 680 g cod fillets, cut into 1-inch strips
- 1 teaspoon salt
- ½ teaspoon freshly ground black pepper
- 2 eggs
- 35 g almond flour
- 20 g grated Parmesan cheese
- Tartar Sauce:
- 120 ml sour cream
- 120 ml mayonnaise
- 3 tablespoons chopped dill pickle
- 2 tablespoons capers, drained and chopped
- ½ teaspoon dried dill
- 1 tablespoon dill gherkin liquid (optional)

1. Preheat the air fryer to 200°C. 2. Season the cod with the salt and black pepper; set aside. 3. In a shallow bowl, lightly beat the eggs. In a second shallow bowl, combine the almond flour and Parmesan cheese. Stir until thoroughly combined. 4. Working with a few pieces at a time, dip the fish into the egg mixture followed by the flour mixture. Press lightly to ensure an even coating. 5. Arrange the fish in a single layer in the air fryer basket and spray lightly with olive oil. Pause halfway through the cooking time to turn the fish. In zone 1, select the AIR FRY button, and set time to 12 to 15 minutes, until the fish flakes easily with a fork. In zone 2, select Match Cook and press Start. Let sit in the basket for a few minutes before serving with the tartar sauce. 6. To make the tartar sauce: In a small bowl, combine the sour cream, mayonnaise, pickle, capers, and dill. If you prefer a thinner sauce, stir in the gherkin liquid.

Chapter 6   Poultry

Celery Chicken

Prep time: 10 minutes | Cook time: 15 minutes | Serves 4

- 120 ml soy sauce
- 2 tablespoons hoisin sauce
- 4 teaspoons minced garlic
- 1 teaspoon freshly ground black pepper
- 8 boneless, skinless chicken tenderloins
- 120 g chopped celery
- 1 medium red pepper, diced
- Olive oil spray

1. Preheat the air fryer to 190°C. Spray the air fryer basket lightly with olive oil spray. 2. In a large bowl, mix together the soy sauce, hoisin sauce, garlic, and black pepper to make a marinade. Add the chicken, celery, and pepper and toss to coat. 3. Shake the excess marinade off the chicken, place it and the vegetables in the air fryer basket, and lightly spray with olive oil spray. Reserve the remaining marinade. 4. In zone 1, select the AIR FRY button, and set time to 4 to 8 minutes. In zone 2, select Match Cook and press Start. Turn the chicken over and brush with some of the remaining marinade. Air fry for an additional 5 to 7 minutes, or until the chicken reaches an internal temperature of at least 76°C. Serve.

Turkish Chicken Kebabs

Prep time: 30 minutes | Cook time: 15 minutes | Serves 4

- 70 g plain Greek yoghurt
- 1 tablespoon minced garlic
- 1 tablespoon tomato paste
- 1 tablespoon fresh lemon juice
- 1 tablespoon vegetable oil
- 1 teaspoon kosher salt
- 1 teaspoon ground cumin
- 1 teaspoon sweet Hungarian paprika
- ½ teaspoon ground cinnamon
- ½ teaspoon black pepper
- ½ teaspoon cayenne pepper
- 450 g boneless, skinless chicken thighs, quartered crosswise

1. In a large bowl, combine the yoghurt, garlic, tomato paste, lemon juice, vegetable oil, salt, cumin, paprika, cinnamon, black pepper, and cayenne. Stir until the spices are blended into the yoghurt. 2. Add the chicken to the bowl and toss until well coated. Marinate at room temperature for 30 minutes, or cover and refrigerate for up to 24 hours. 3. Arrange the chicken in a single layer in the air fryer basket. In zone 1, select the AIR FRY button, adjust temperature to 190°C, set time to 10 minutes. In zone 2, select Match Cook and press Start. Turn the chicken and cook for 5 minutes more. Use a meat thermometer to ensure the chicken has reached an internal temperature of 76°C.

Spanish Chicken and Mini Sweet Pepper Baguette

Prep time: 10 minutes | Cook time: 20 minutes | Serves 2

- 570 g assorted small chicken parts, breasts cut into halves
- ¼ teaspoon salt
- ¼ teaspoon ground black pepper
- 2 teaspoons olive oil
- 230 g mini sweet peppers
- 60 g light mayonnaise
- ¼ teaspoon smoked paprika
- ½ clove garlic, crushed
- Baguette, for serving
- Cooking spray

1. Preheat air fryer to 190ºC. Spritz the air fryer basket with cooking spray. 2. Toss the chicken with salt, ground black pepper, and olive oil in a large bowl. 3. Arrange the sweet peppers and chicken in the preheated air fryer. In zone 1, select the AIR FRY button, and set time to 10 minutes. In zone 2, select Match Cook and press Start. Then transfer the peppers on a plate. 4. Flip the chicken and air fry for 10 more minutes or until well browned. 5. Meanwhile, combine the mayo, paprika, and garlic in a small bowl. Stir to mix well. 6. Assemble the baguette with chicken and sweet pepper, then spread with mayo mixture and serve.

Curried Orange Honey Chicken

Prep time: 10 minutes | Cook time: 16 to 19 minutes | Serves 4

- 340 g boneless, skinless chicken thighs, cut into 1-inch pieces
- 1 yellow pepper, cut into 1½-inch pieces
- 1 small red onion, sliced
- Olive oil for misting
- 60 ml chicken stock
- 2 tablespoons honey
- 60 ml orange juice
- 1 tablespoon cornflour
- 2 to 3 teaspoons curry powder

1. Preheat the air fryer to 190ºC. 2. Put the chicken thighs, pepper, and red onion in the air fryer basket and mist with olive oil. 3. In zone 1, select the ROAST button, and set time to 12 to 12 minutes or until the chicken is cooked to 76ºC, shaking the basket halfway through cooking time. In zone 2, select Match Cook and press Start. 4. Remove the chicken and vegetables from the air fryer basket and set aside. 5. In a metal bowl, combine the stock, honey, orange juice, cornflour, and curry powder, and mix well. Add the chicken and vegetables, stir, and put the bowl in the basket. 6. Return the basket to the air fryer and roast for 2 minutes. Remove and stir, then roast for 2 to 3 minutes or until the sauce is thickened and bubbly. 7. Serve warm.

South Indian Pepper Chicken

Prep time: 30 minutes | Cook time: 15 minutes | Serves 4

Spice Mix:
- 1 dried red chilli, or ½ teaspoon dried red pepper flakes
- 1-inch piece cinnamon or cassia bark
- 1½ teaspoons coriander seeds
- 1 teaspoon fennel seeds
- 1 teaspoon cumin seeds
- 1 teaspoon black pepper maize
- ½ teaspoon cardamom seeds
- ¼ teaspoon ground turmeric
- 1 teaspoon kosher salt

Chicken:
- 450 g boneless, skinless chicken thighs, cut crosswise into thirds
- 2 medium onions, cut into ½-inch-thick slices
- 60 ml olive oil
- Cauliflower rice, steamed rice, or naan bread, for serving

1. For the spice mix: Combine the dried chilli, cinnamon, coriander, fennel, cumin, peppercorns, and cardamom in a clean coffee or spice grinder. Grind, shaking the grinder lightly so all the seeds and bits get into the blades, until the mixture is broken down to a fine powder. Stir in the turmeric and salt. 2. For the chicken: Place the chicken and onions in resealable plastic bag. Add the oil and 1½ tablespoons of the spice mix. Seal the bag and massage until the chicken is well coated. Marinate at room temperature for 30 minutes or in the refrigerator for up to 24 hours. 3. Place the chicken and onions in the air fryer basket. In zone 1, select the AIR FRY button, adjust temperature to 180ºC, set time to 10 minutes. In zone 2, select Match Cook and press Start, stirring once halfway through the cooking time. Increase the temperature to 200ºC for 5 minutes. Use a meat thermometer to ensure the chicken has reached an internal temperature of 76ºC. 4. Serve with steamed rice, cauliflower rice, or naan.

Pepper Stuffed Chicken Roll-Ups

Prep time: 10 minutes | Cook time: 12 minutes | Serves 4

- 2 (115 g) boneless, skinless chicken breasts, slice in half horizontally
- 1 tablespoon olive oil
- Juice of ½ lime
- 2 tablespoons taco seasoning
- ½ green pepper, cut into strips
- ½ red pepper, cut into strips
- ¼ onion, sliced

1. Preheat the air fryer to 200ºC. 2. Unfold the chicken breast slices on a clean work surface. Rub with olive oil, then drizzle with lime juice and sprinkle with taco seasoning. 3. Top the chicken slices with equal amount of peppers and onion. Roll them up and secure with toothpicks. 4. Arrange the chicken roll-ups in the preheated air fryer. In zone 1, select the AIR FRY button, and set time to 12 minutes or until the internal temperature of the chicken reaches at least 76ºC. In zone 2, select Match Cook and press Start. Flip the chicken roll-ups halfway through. 5. Remove the chicken from the air fryer. Discard the toothpicks and serve immediately.

Garlic Parmesan Drumsticks

Prep time: 5 minutes | Cook time: 25 minutes | Serves 4

- 8 (115 g) chicken drumsticks
- ½ teaspoon salt
- ⅛ teaspoon ground black pepper
- ½ teaspoon garlic powder
- 2 tablespoons salted butter, melted
- 45 g grated Parmesan cheese
- 1 tablespoon dried parsley

1. Sprinkle drumsticks with salt, pepper, and garlic powder. Place drumsticks into ungreased air fryer basket. 2. In zone 1, select the AIR FRY button, adjust temperature to 200ºC, set time to 25 minutes. In zone 2, select Match Cook and press Start, turning drumsticks halfway through cooking. Drumsticks will be golden and have an internal temperature of at least 76ºC when done. 3. Transfer drumsticks to a large serving dish. Pour butter over drumsticks, and sprinkle with Parmesan and parsley. Serve warm.

Chicken Thighs in Waffles

Prep time: 1 hour 20 minutes | Cook time: 40 minutes | Serves 4

For the chicken:

- 4 chicken thighs, skin on
- 240 ml low-fat buttermilk
- 35 g plain flour
- ½ teaspoon garlic powder
- ½ teaspoon mustard powder
- 1 teaspoon kosher salt
- ½ teaspoon freshly ground black pepper
- 85 g honey, for serving
- Cooking spray

For the waffles:

- 35 g plain flour
- 35 g whole wheat pastry flour
- 1 large egg, beaten
- 240 ml low-fat buttermilk
- 1 teaspoon baking powder
- 2 tablespoons rapeseed oil
- ½ teaspoon kosher salt
- 1 tablespoon granulated sugar

1. Combine the chicken thighs with buttermilk in a large bowl. Wrap the bowl in plastic and refrigerate to marinate for at least an hour. 2. Preheat the air fryer to 180ºC. Spritz the air fryer basket with cooking spray. 3. Combine the flour, mustard powder, garlic powder, salt, and black pepper in a shallow dish. Stir to mix well. 4. Remove the thighs from the buttermilk and pat dry with paper towels. Sit the bowl of buttermilk aside. 5. Dip the thighs in the flour mixture first, then into the buttermilk, and then into the flour mixture. Shake the excess off. 6. Arrange the thighs in the preheated air fryer and spritz with cooking spray. In zone 1, select the AIR FRY button, and set time to 20 minutes or until an instant-read thermometer inserted in the thickest part of the chicken thighs registers at least 76ºC. In zone 2, select Match Cook and press Start. Flip the thighs halfway through. 7. Meanwhile, make the waffles: combine the ingredients for the waffles in a large bowl. Stir to mix well, then arrange the mixture in a waffle iron and cook until a golden and fragrant waffle forms. 8. Remove the waffles from the waffle iron and slice into 4 pieces. Remove the chicken thighs from the air fryer and allow to cool for 5 minutes. 9. Arrange each chicken thigh on each waffle piece and drizzle with 1 tablespoon of honey. Serve warm.

Chicken Legs with Leeks

Prep time: 30 minutes | Cook time: 18 minutes | Serves 6

- 2 leeks, sliced
- 2 large-sized tomatoes, chopped
- 3 cloves garlic, minced
- ½ teaspoon dried oregano
- 6 chicken legs, boneless and skinless
- ½ teaspoon smoked cayenne pepper
- 2 tablespoons olive oil
- A freshly ground nutmeg

1. In a mixing dish, thoroughly combine all ingredients, minus the leeks. Place in the refrigerator and let it marinate overnight. 2. Lay the leeks onto the bottom of the air fryer basket. Top with the chicken legs. 3. In zone 1, select the ROAST button, adjust temperature to 190ºC, set time to 10 minutes. In zone 2, select Match Cook and press Start, turning halfway through. Serve with hoisin sauce.

Sesame Chicken Breast

Prep time: 10 minutes | Cook time: 18 minutes | Serves 6

- Oil, for spraying
- 2 (170 g) boneless, skinless chicken breasts, cut into bite-size pieces
- 30 g cornflour plus 1 tablespoon
- 60 ml soy sauce
- 2 tablespoons packed light brown sugar
- 2 tablespoons pineapple juice
- 1 tablespoon black treacle
- ½ teaspoon ground ginger
- 1 tablespoon water
- 2 teaspoons sesame seeds

1. Line the air fryer basket with parchment and spray lightly with oil. 2. Place the chicken and 60 g of cornflour in a zip-top plastic bag, seal, and shake well until evenly coated. 3. Place the chicken in an even layer in the prepared basket and spray liberally with oil. 4. In zone 1, select the AIR FRY button, adjust temperature to 200ºC, set time to 9 minutes. In zone 2, select Match Cook and press Start. Flip, spray with more oil, and cook for another 8 to 9 minutes, or until the internal temperature reaches 76ºC. 5. In a small saucepan, combine the soy sauce, brown sugar, pineapple juice, black treacle, and ginger over medium heat and cook, stirring frequently, until the brown sugar has dissolved. 6. In a small bowl, mix together the water and remaining 1 tablespoon of cornflour. Pour it into the soy sauce mixture. 7. Bring the mixture to a boil, stirring frequently, until the sauce thickens. Remove from the heat. 8. Transfer the chicken to a large bowl, add the sauce, and toss until evenly coated. Sprinkle with the sesame seeds and serve.

Golden Tenders

Prep time: 10 minutes | Cook time: 15 minutes | Serves 4

- 60 g panko bread crumbs
- 1 tablespoon paprika
- ½ teaspoon salt
- ¼ teaspoon freshly ground black pepper
- 16 chicken tenders
- 115 g mayonnaise
- Olive oil spray

1. In a medium bowl, stir together the panko, paprika, salt, and pepper. 2. In a large bowl, toss together the chicken tenders and mayonnaise to coat. Transfer the coated chicken pieces to the bowl of seasoned panko and dredge to coat thoroughly. Press the coating onto the chicken with your fingers. 3. Insert the crisper plate into the basket and the basket into the unit. Preheat the unit by selecting AIR FRY, setting the temperature to 180°C, and setting the time to 3 minutes. Select START/STOP to begin. 4. Once the unit is preheated, place a parchment paper liner into the basket. Place the chicken into the basket and spray it with olive oil. 5. In zone 1, select the AIR FRY button, adjust temperature to 180°C, set time to 15 minutes. In zone 2, select Match Cook and press Start. 6. When the cooking is complete, the tenders will be golden brown and a food thermometer inserted into the chicken should register 76°C. For more even browning, remove the basket halfway through cooking and flip the tenders. Give them an extra spray of olive oil and reinsert the basket to resume cooking. This ensures they are crispy and brown all over. 7. When the cooking is complete, serve.

Chicken Pesto Pizzas

Prep time: 10 minutes | Cook time: 12 minutes | Serves 4

- 450 g chicken mince thighs
- ¼ teaspoon salt
- ⅛ teaspoon ground black pepper
- 20 g basil pesto
- 225 g shredded Mozzarella cheese
- 4 grape tomatoes, sliced

1. Cut four squares of parchment paper to fit into your air fryer basket. 2. Place chicken mince in a large bowl and mix with salt and pepper. Divide mixture into four equal sections. 3. Wet your hands with water to prevent sticking, then press each section into a 6-inch circle onto a piece of ungreased parchment. Place each chicken crust into air fryer basket, working in batches if needed. 4. In zone 1, select the AIR FRY button, adjust temperature to 180°C, set time to 10 minutes. In zone 2, select Match Cook and press Start, turning crusts halfway through cooking. 5. Spread 1 tablespoon pesto across the top of each crust, then sprinkle with ¼ of the Mozzarella and top with 1 sliced tomato. Continue cooking at 180°C for 2 minutes. Cheese will be melted and brown when done. Serve warm.

Cranberry Curry Chicken

Prep time: 12 minutes | Cook time: 18 minutes | Serves 4

- 3 (140 g) low-sodium boneless, skinless chicken breasts, cut into 1½-inch cubes
- 2 teaspoons olive oil
- 2 tablespoons cornflour
- 1 tablespoon curry powder
- 1 tart apple, chopped
- 120 ml low-sodium chicken broth
- 60 g dried cranberries
- 2 tablespoons freshly squeezed orange juice
- Brown rice, cooked (optional)

1. Preheat the air fryer to 196ºC. 2. In a medium bowl, mix the chicken and olive oil. Sprinkle with the cornflour and curry powder. Toss to coat. Stir in the apple and transfer to a metal pan. In zone 1, select the BAKE button, and set time to 8 minutes. In zone 2, select Match Cook and press Start, stirring once during cooking. 3. Add the chicken broth, cranberries, and orange juice. Bake for about 10 minutes more, or until the sauce is slightly thickened and the chicken reaches an internal temperature of 76ºC on a meat thermometer. Serve over hot cooked brown rice, if desired.

Chicken Rochambeau

Prep time: 15 minutes | Cook time: 20 minutes | Serves 4

- 1 tablespoon butter
- 4 chicken tenders, cut in half crosswise
- Salt and pepper, to taste
- 2 tablespoons butter
- 25 g chopped spring onions
- 50 g chopped mushrooms
- 15 g flour
- Oil for misting
- 4 slices gammon, ¼- to ⅜-inches thick

Sauce:
- 2 tablespoons flour
- 240 ml chicken broth
- ¼ teaspoon garlic powder
- and large enough to cover an English muffin
- 2 English muffins, split
- 1½ teaspoons Worcestershire sauce

1. Place 1 tablespoon of butter in a baking pan and air fry at 200ºC for 2 minutes to melt. 2. Sprinkle chicken tenders with salt and pepper to taste, then roll in the flour. 3. Place chicken in baking pan, turning pieces to coat with melted butter. 4. In zone 1, select the AIR FRY button, adjust temperature to 200ºC, set time to 5 minutes. In zone 2, select Match Cook and press Start. Turn chicken pieces over, and spray tops lightly with olive oil. Cook 5 minutes longer or until juices run clear. The chicken will not brown. 5. While chicken is cooking, make the sauce: In a medium saucepan, melt the 2 tablespoons of butter. 6. Add onions and mushrooms and sauté until tender, about 3 minutes. 7. Stir in the flour. Gradually add broth, stirring constantly until you have a smooth gravy. 8. Add garlic powder and Worcestershire sauce and simmer on low heat until sauce thickens, about 5 minutes. 9. When chicken is cooked, remove baking pan from air fryer and set aside. 10. Place gammon slices directly into air fryer basket and air fry at 200ºC for 5 minutes or until hot and beginning to sizzle a little. Remove and set aside on top of the chicken for now. 11. Place the English muffin halves in air fryer basket and air fry at 200ºC for 1 minute. 12. Open air fryer and place a gammon slice on top of each English muffin half. Stack 2 pieces of chicken on top of each gammon slice. Air fry for 1 to 2 minutes to heat through. 13. Place each English muffin stack on a serving plate and top with plenty of sauce.

Cheese-Encrusted Chicken Tenderloins with Peanuts

Prep time: 10 minutes | Cook time: 25 minutes | Serves 4

- 45 g grated Parmesan cheese
- ½ teaspoon garlic powder
- 1 teaspoon red pepper flakes
- Sea salt and ground black pepper, to taste
- 2 tablespoons peanut oil
- 680 g chicken tenderloins
- 2 tablespoons peanuts, roasted and roughly chopped
- Cooking spray

1. Preheat the air fryer to 180ºC. Spritz the air fryer basket with cooking spray. 2. Combine the Parmesan cheese, garlic powder, red pepper flakes, salt, black pepper, and peanut oil in a large bowl. Stir to mix well. 3. Dip the chicken tenderloins in the cheese mixture, then press to coat well. Shake the excess off. 4. Transfer the chicken tenderloins in the air fryer basket. In zone 1, select the AIR FRY button, and set time to 12 minutes or until well browned. In zone 2, select Match Cook and press Start. Flip the tenderloin halfway through. You may need to work in batches to avoid overcrowding. 5. Transfer the chicken tenderloins on a large plate and top with roasted peanuts before serving.

Easy Chicken Fingers

Prep time: 20 minutes | Cook time: 30 minutes | Makes 12 chicken fingers

- 30 g plain flour
- 120 g panko breadcrumbs
- 2 tablespoons rapeseed oil
- 1 large egg
- 3 boneless and skinless chicken breasts, each cut into 4 strips
- Coarse salt and freshly ground black pepper, to taste
- Cooking spray

1. Preheat the air fryer to 180ºC. Spritz the air fryer basket with cooking spray. 2. Pour the flour in a large bowl. Combine the panko and rapeseed oil on a shallow dish. Whisk the egg in a separate bowl. 3. Rub the chicken strips with salt and ground black pepper on a clean work surface, then dip the chicken in the bowl of flour. Shake the excess off and dunk the chicken strips in the bowl of whisked egg, then roll the strips over the panko to coat well. 4. Arrange 4 strips in the air fryer basket each time and air fry for 10 minutes or until crunchy and lightly browned. Flip the strips halfway through. Repeat with remaining ingredients. 5. Serve immediately.

Chapter 7   Snacks and Starters

Dark Chocolate and Cranberry Muesli Bars

Prep time: 5 minutes | Cook time: 15 minutes | Serves 6

- 135 g certified gluten-free quick oats
- 2 tablespoons sugar-free dark chocolate chunks
- 2 tablespoons unsweetened dried cranberries
- 3 tablespoons unsweetened desiccated coconut
- 120 ml raw honey
- 1 teaspoon cinnamon powder
- ⅛ teaspoon salt
- 2 tablespoons olive oil

1. Preheat the air fryer to 180ºC. Line an 8-by-8-inch baking dish with baking paper paper that comes up the side so you tin lift it out after cooking. 2. In a large bowl, mix together all of the ingredients until well combined. 3. Press the oat mixture into the pans in an even layer. 4. Place the pans into the air fryer basket. In zone 1, select the BAKE button, and set time to 15 minutes. In zone 2, select Match Cook and press Start. 5. Remove the pans from the air fryer and lift the muesli cake out of the pan using the edges of the baking paper paper. 6. Allow to cool for 5 minutes before slicing into 6 equal bars. 7. Serve immediately or wrap in cling film and store at room temperature for up to 1 week.

Browned Ricotta with Capers and Lemon

Prep time: 10 minutes | Cook time: 8 to 10 minutes | Serves 4 to 6

- 320 g whole milk ricotta cheese
- 2 tablespoons extra-virgin olive oil
- 2 tablespoons capers, rinsed
- Zest of 1 lemon, plus more for garnish
- 1 teaspoon finely chopped fresh rosemary
- Pinch crushed red pepper flakes
- Salt and freshly ground black pepper, to taste
- 1 tablespoon grated Parmesan cheese

1. Preheat the air fryer to 190ºC. 2. In a mixing bowl, stir together the ricotta cheese, olive oil, capers, lemon zest, rosemary, red pepper flakes, salt, and pepper until well combined. 3. Spread the mixture evenly in a baking dish and place it in the air fryer basket. 4. In zone 1, select the AIR FRY button, and set time to 8 to 10 minutes until the top is nicely browned. In zone 2, select Match Cook and press Start. 5. Remove from the basket and top with a sprinkle of grated Parmesan cheese. 6. Garnish with the lemon zest and serve warm.

Cheese Drops

Prep time: 15 minutes | Cook time: 10 minutes per batch | Serves 8

- 90 g plain flour
- ½ teaspoon rock salt
- ¼ teaspoon cayenne pepper
- ¼ teaspoon smoked paprika
- ¼ teaspoon black pepper
- a dash of garlic powder (optional)
- 57 g butter, softened
- 100 g grated extra mature cheddar cheese, at room temperature
- Olive oil spray

1. In a small bowl, combine the flour, salt, cayenne, paprika, pepper, and garlic powder, if using. 2. Using a food processor, cream the butter and cheese until smooth. Gently add the seasoned flour and process until the dough is well combined, smooth, and no longer sticky. (Or make the dough in a stand mixer fitted with the paddle attachment: Cream the butter and cheese at medium speed until smooth, then add the seasoned flour and beat at low speed until smooth.) 3. Divide the dough into 32 pieces of equal size. On a lightly floured surface, roll each piece into a small ball. 4. Spray the air fryer basket with oil spray. Arrange 16 cheese drops in the basket. In zone 1, select the AIR FRY button, adjust temperature to 160ºC, set time to 10 minutes, or until drops are just starting to brown. In zone 2, select Match Cook and press Start. Transfer to a a wire rack. Repeat with remaining dough, checking for degree of doneness at 8 minutes. 5. Cool the cheese drops completely on the a wire rack. Store in an airtight container until ready to serve, or up to 1 or 2 days.

Roasted Pearl Onion Dip

Prep time: 5 minutes | Cook time: 12 minutes | Serves 4

- 275 g peeled pearl onions
- 3 garlic cloves
- 3 tablespoons olive oil, divided
- ½ teaspoon salt
- 240 ml non-fat plain Greek yoghurt
- 1 tablespoon lemon juice
- ¼ teaspoon black pepper
- ⅛ teaspoon red pepper flakes
- Pitta chips, mixed vegetables, or toasted bread for serving (optional)

1. Preheat the air fryer to 180ºC. 2. In a large bowl, combine the pearl onions and garlic with 2 tablespoons of the olive oil until the onions are well coated. 3. Pour the garlic-and-onion mixture into the air fryer basket. In zone 1, select the ROAST button, and set time to 12 minutes. In zone 2, select Match Cook and press Start. 4. Transfer the garlic and onions to a food processor. Pulse the mixed vegetables several times, until the onions are minced but still have some chunks. 5. In a large bowl, combine the garlic and onions and the remaining 1 tablespoon of olive oil, along with the salt, yoghurt, lemon juice, black pepper, and red pepper flakes. 6. Cover and chill for 1 hour before serving with pitta chips, mixed vegetables, or toasted bread.

Golden Onion Rings

Prep time: 15 minutes | Cook time: 14 minutes per batch | Serves 4

- 1 large white onion, peeled and cut into ½ to ¾-inch-thick slices (about 475 g)
- 120 ml semi-skimmed milk
- 115 g wholemeal pastry flour, or plain flour
- 2 tablespoons cornflour
- ¾ teaspoon sea salt, divided
- ½ teaspoon freshly ground black pepper, divided
- ¾ teaspoon garlic powder, divided
- 110 g wholemeal breadcrumbs, or gluten-free breadcrumbs
- Cooking oil spray (coconut, sunflower, or safflower)
- tomato ketchup, for serving (optional)

1. Carefully separate the onion slices into rings—a gentle touch is important here. 2. Place the milk in a shallow dish and set aside. 3. Make the first breading: In a medium-sized bowl, stir together the flour, cornflour, ¼ teaspoon of salt, ¼ teaspoon of pepper, and ¼ teaspoon of garlic powder. Set aside. 4. Make the second breading: In a separate medium bowl, stir together the breadcrumbs with the remaining ½ teaspoon of salt, the remaining ½ teaspoon of garlic, and the remaining ½ teaspoon of pepper. Set aside. 5. Insert the crisper plate into the basket and the basket into the unit. Preheat the unit by selecting AIR FRY, setting the temperature to 200ºC, and setting the time to 3 minutes. Select START/STOP to begin. 6. Once the unit is preheated, spray the crisper plate and the basket with cooking oil. 7. To make the onion rings, dip one ring into the milk and into the first breading mixture. Dip the ring into the milk again and back into the first breading mixture, coating thoroughly. Dip the ring into the milk one last time and then into the second breading mixture, coating thoroughly. Gently lay the onion ring in the basket. Repeat with additional rings and, as you place them into the basket, do not overlap them too much. Once all the onion rings are in the basket, generously spray the tops with cooking oil. 8. In zone 1, select the AIR FRY button, adjust temperature to 200ºC, set time to 14 minutes. In zone 2, select Match Cook and press Start. 9. After 4 minutes, open the unit and spray the rings generously with cooking oil. Close the unit to resume cooking. After 3 minutes, remove the basket and spray the onion rings again. Remove the rings, turn them over, and place them back into the basket. Generously spray them again with oil. Reinsert the basket to resume cooking. After 4 minutes, generously spray the rings with oil one last time. Resume cooking for the remaining 3 minutes, or until the onion rings are very crunchy and brown. 10. When the cooking is complete, serve the hot rings with tomato ketchup, or other sauce of choice.

Roasted Mushrooms with Garlic

Prep time: 3 minutes | Cook time: 22 to 27 minutes | Serves 4

- 16 garlic cloves, peeled
- 2 teaspoons olive oil, divided
- 16 button mushrooms
- ½ teaspoon dried marjoram
- ⅛ teaspoon freshly ground black pepper
- 1 tablespoon white wine or low-salt mixed vegetables broth

1. In a baking pan, mix the garlic with 1 teaspoon of olive oil. In zone 1, select the ROAST button, adjust temperature to 180ºC, set time to 12 minutes. In zone 2, select Match Cook and press Start. 2. Add the mushrooms, marjoram, and pepper. Stir to coat. Drizzle with the remaining 1 teaspoon of olive oil and the white wine. 3. Return to the air fryer and roast for 10 to 15 minutes more, or until the mushrooms and garlic cloves are tender. Serve.

Tangy Fried A Gherkin Spears

Prep time: 5 minutes | Cook time: 15 minutes | Serves 6

- 2 jars sweet and sour a pickled gherkin spears, patted dry
- 2 medium-sized eggs
- 80 ml milk
- 1 teaspoon garlic powder
- 1 teaspoon sea salt
- ½ teaspoon shallot powder
- ⅓ teaspoon chilli powder
- 80 g plain flour
- Cooking spray

1. Preheat the air fryer to 200ºC. Spritz the air fryer basket with cooking spray. 2. In a bowl, beat together the eggs with milk. In another bowl, combine garlic powder, sea salt, shallot powder, chilli powder and plain flour until well blended. 3. One by one, roll the a pickled gherkin spears in the powder mixture, then dredge them in the egg mixture. Dip them in the powder mixture a second time for additional coating. 4. Arrange the coated pickled cucumbers in the prepared basket. In zone 1, select the AIR FRY button, and set time to 15 minutes. In zone 2, select Match Cook and press Start. Air fry until golden and crispy, shaking the basket halfway through to ensure even cooking. 5. Transfer to a plate and let cool for 5 minutes before serving.

Lemony Endive in Curried Yoghurt

Prep time: 5 minutes | Cook time: 10 minutes | Serves 6

- 6 heads endive
- 120 ml plain and fat-free yoghurt
- 3 tablespoons lemon juice
- 1 teaspoon garlic powder
- ½ teaspoon curry powder
- Salt and ground black pepper, to taste

1. Wash the endives and slice them in half lengthwise. 2. In a bowl, mix together the yoghurt, lemon juice, garlic powder, curry powder, salt and pepper. 3. Brush the endive halves with the marinade, coating them completely. Allow to sit for at least 30 minutes or up to 24 hours. 4. Preheat the air fryer to 160ºC. 5. Put the endives in the air fryer basket. In zone 1, select the AIR FRY button, and set time to 10 minutes. In zone 2, select Match Cook and press Start. 6. Serve hot.

Chilli-brined Fried Calamari

Prep time: 20 minutes | Cook time: 8 minutes | Serves 2

- 1 (227 g) jar sweet or hot pickled cherry peppers
- 227 g calamari bodies and tentacles, bodies cut into ½-inch-wide rings
- 1 lemon
- 200 g plain flour
- Rock salt and freshly ground black pepper, to taste
- 3 large eggs, lightly beaten
- Cooking spray
- 120 ml mayonnaise
- 1 teaspoon finely chopped rosemary
- 1 garlic clove, minced

1. Drain the pickled pepper brine into a large bowl and tear the peppers into bite-size strips. Add the pepper strips and calamari to the brine and let stand in the refrigerator for 20 minutes or up to 2 hours. 2. Grate the lemon zest into a large bowl then whisk in the flour and season with salt and pepper. Dip the calamari and pepper strips in the egg, then toss them in the flour mixture until fully coated. Spray the calamari and peppers liberally with cooking spray, then transfer half to the air fryer. In zone 1, select the AIR FRY button, adjust temperature to 200ºC, set time to 8 minutes. In zone 2, select Match Cook and press Start, shaking the basket halfway into cooking, until the calamari is fully cooked and golden. Transfer to a plate and repeat with the remaining pieces. 3. In a small bowl, whisk together the mayonnaise, rosemary, and garlic. Squeeze half the zested lemon to get 1 tablespoon of juice and stir it into the sauce. Season with salt and pepper. Cut the remaining zested lemon half into 4 small wedges and serve alongside the calamari, peppers, and sauce.

Red Pepper Tapenade

Prep time: 5 minutes | Cook time: 5 minutes | Serves 4

- 1 large red pepper
- 2 tablespoons plus 1 teaspoon olive oil, divided
- 120 g Kalamata olives, pitted and roughly chopped
- 1 garlic clove, minced
- ½ teaspoon dried oregano
- 1 tablespoon lemon juice

1. Preheat the air fryer to 190ºC. 2. Brush the outside of a whole red pepper with 1 teaspoon olive oil and place it inside the air fryer basket. In zone 1, select the ROAST button, and set time to 5 minutes. In zone 2, select Match Cook and press Start. 3. Meanwhile, in a medium-sized bowl combine the remaining 2 tablespoons of olive oil with the olives, garlic, oregano, and lemon juice. 4. Remove the red pepper from the air fryer, then gently slice off the stem and remove the seeds. Roughly chop the roasted pepper into small pieces. 5. Add the red pepper to the olive mixture and stir all together until combined. 6. Serve with pitta chips, crackers, or crusty bread.

Shishito Peppers with Herb Dressing

Prep time: 10 minutes | Cook time: 6 minutes | Serves 2 to 4

- 170 g shishito or Padron peppers
- 1 tablespoon mixed vegetables oil
- Rock salt and freshly ground black pepper, to taste
- 120 ml mayonnaise
- 2 tablespoons finely chopped fresh basil leaves
- 2 tablespoons finely chopped fresh flat-leaf parsley parsley
- 1 tablespoon finely chopped fresh tarragon
- 1 tablespoon finely finely chopped fresh chives
- Finely grated zest of ½ lemon
- 1 tablespoon fresh lemon juice
- Flaky sea salt, for serving

1. Preheat the air fryer to 200ºC. 2. In a bowl, toss together the shishitos and oil to evenly coat and season with rock salt and black pepper. Transfer to the air fryer. In zone 1, select the AIR FRY button, and set time to 6 minutes. In zone 2, select Match Cook and press Start, shaking the basket halfway through, or until the shishitos are blistered and lightly charred. 3. Meanwhile, in a small bowl, whisk together the mayonnaise, basil, parsley, tarragon, chives, lemon zest, and lemon juice. 4. Pile the peppers on a plate, sprinkle with flaky sea salt, and serve hot with the dressing.

Mexican Potato Skins

Prep time: 10 minutes | Cook time: 55 minutes | Serves 6

- Olive oil
- 6 medium russet potatoes or Maris Piper potatoes, scrubbed
- Salt and freshly ground black pepper, to taste
- 260 g fat-free refried black beans
- 1 tablespoon taco seasoning
- 120 g salsa
- 80 g low-fat shredded Cheddar cheese

1. Spray the air fryer basket lightly with olive oil. 2. Spray the potatoes lightly with oil and season with salt and pepper. Pierce each potato a few times with a fork. 3. Place the potatoes in the air fryer basket. In zone 1, select the AIR FRY button, adjust temperature to 200ºC, set time to 30 to 40 minutes until fork-tender. In zone 2, select Match Cook and press Start.The cooking time will depend on the size of the potatoes. You tin cook the potatoes in the microwave or a standard oven, but they won't get the same lovely crispy skin they will get in the air fryer. 4. While the potatoes are cooking, in a small bowl, mix together the beans and taco seasoning. Set aside until the potatoes are cool enough to handle. 5. Cut each potato in half lengthwise. Scoop out most of the insides, leaving about ¼ inch in the skins so the potato skins hold their shape. 6. Season the insides of the potato skins with salt and black pepper. Lightly spray the insides of the potato skins with oil. 7. Place them into the air fryer basket, skin-side down, and air fry until crisp and golden, 8 to 10 minutes. 8. Transfer the skins to a work surface and spoon ½ tablespoon of seasoned refried black beans into each one. Top each with 2 teaspoons salsa and 1 tablespoon shredded Cheddar cheese. 9. Place filled potato skins in the air fryer basket in a single layer. Lightly spray with oil. 10. Air fry until the cheese is melted and bubbly, 2 to 3 minutes.

Stuffed Fried Mushrooms

Prep time: 20 minutes | Cook time: 10 to 11 minutes | Serves 10

- 50 g panko breadcrumbs
- ½ teaspoon freshly ground black pepper
- ½ teaspoon onion powder
- ½ teaspoon cayenne pepper
- 1 (227 g) package soft white cheese, at room temperature
- 20 cremini or button mushrooms, stemmed
- 1 to 2 tablespoons oil

1. In a medium-sized bowl, whisk the breadcrumbs, black pepper, onion powder, and cayenne until blended. 2. Add the soft white cheese and mix until well blended. Fill each mushroom top with 1 teaspoon of the soft white cheese mixture 3. Preheat the air fryer to 180ºC. Line the air fryer basket with a piece of baking paper paper. 4. Place the mushrooms on the baking paper and spritz with oil. 5. In zone 1, select the AIR FRY button, and set time to 5 minutes. In zone 2, select Match Cook and press Start. Shake the basket and cook for 5 to 6 minutes more until the filling is firm and the mushrooms are soft.

Cheesy Steak Fries

Prep time: 5 minutes | Cook time: 20 minutes | Serves 5

- 1 (794 g) bag frozen chunky chips
- Cooking spray
- Salt and pepper, to taste
- 120 ml beef gravy
- 90 g shredded mozzarella cheese cheese
- 2 spring onions, green parts only, chopped

1. Preheat the air fryer to 200ºC. 2. Place the frozen chunky chips in the air fryer. In zone 1, select the AIR FRY button, and set time to 10 minutes. In zone 2, select Match Cook and press Start. Shake the basket and spritz the fries with cooking spray. Sprinkle with salt and pepper. Air fry for an additional 8 minutes. 3. Pour the beef gravy into a medium, microwave-safe bowl. Microwave for 30 seconds, or until the gravy is warm. 4. Sprinkle the fries with the cheese. Air fry for an additional 2 minutes, until the cheese is melted. 5. Transfer the fries to a serving dish. Drizzle the fries with gravy and sprinkle the spring onions on top for a green garnish. Serve.

Chapter 8　Desserts

Cream-Filled Sponge Cakes

Prep time: 10 minutes | Cook time: 10 minutes | Makes 4 cakes

- Coconut, or avocado oil, for spraying
- 1 tube croissant dough
- 4 Swiss rolls
- 1 tablespoon icing sugar

1. Line the air fryer basket with baking paper, and spray lightly with oil. 2. Unroll the dough into a single flat layer and cut it into 4 equal pieces. 3. Place 1 sponge cake in the center of each piece of dough. Wrap the dough around the cake, pinching the ends to seal. 4. Place the wrapped cakes in the prepared basket, and spray lightly with oil. 5. In zone 1, select the BAKE button, adjust temperature to 90°C, set time to 5 minutes. In zone 2, select Match Cook and press Start. Flip, spray with oil, and cook for another 5 minutes, or until golden brown. 6. Dust with the icing sugar and serve.

Caramelized Fruit Skewers

Prep time: 10 minutes | Cook time: 3 to 5 minutes | Serves 4

- 2 peaches, peeled, pitted, and thickly sliced
- 3 plums, halved and pitted
- 3 nectarines, halved and pitted
- 1 tablespoon honey
- ½ teaspoon ground cinnamon
- ¼ teaspoon ground allspice
- Pinch cayenne pepper
- Special Equipment:
- 8 metal skewers

1. Preheat the air fryer to 200°C. 2. Thread, alternating peaches, plums, and nectarines, onto the metal skewers that fit into the air fryer. 3. Thoroughly combine the honey, cinnamon, allspice, and cayenne in a small bowl. Brush the glaze generously over the fruit skewers. 4. Transfer the fruit skewers to the air fryer basket. 5. In zone 1, select the AIR FRY button, and set time to 3 to 5 minutes, or until the fruit is caramelized. In zone 2, select Match Cook and press Start. 6. Remove from the basket and repeat with the remaining fruit skewers. 7. Let the fruit skewers rest for 5 minutes before serving.

Chocolate Bread Pudding

Prep time: 10 minutes | Cook time: 10 to 12 minutes | Serves 4

- Nonstick, flour-infused baking spray
- 1 egg
- 1 egg yolk
- 175 ml chocolate milk
- 2 tablespoons cocoa powder
- 3 tablespoons light brown sugar
- 3 tablespoons peanut butter
- 1 teaspoon vanilla extract
- 5 slices firm white bread, cubed

1. Spray a 6-by-2-inch round baking pan with the baking spray. Set aside. 2. In a medium bowl, whisk the egg, egg yolk, chocolate milk, cocoa powder, brown sugar, peanut butter, and vanilla until thoroughly combined. Stir in the bread cubes and let soak for 10 minutes. Spoon this mixture into the prepared pan. 3. Insert the crisper plate into the basket and the basket into the unit. Preheat the unit to 160ºC. 4. Cook the pudding for about 10 minutes and then check if done. It is done when it is firm to the touch. If not, resume cooking. 5. When the cooking is complete, let the pudding cool for 5 minutes. Serve warm.

Lush Chocolate Chip Cookies

Prep time: 7 minutes | Cook time: 9 minutes | Serves 4

- 3 tablespoons butter, at room temperature
- 50 g light brown sugar, plus 1 tablespoon
- 1 egg yolk
- 35 g Plain flour
- 2 tablespoons ground white chocolate
- ¼ teaspoon baking soda
- ½ teaspoon vanilla extract
- 120 g semisweet chocolate crisps
- Nonstick flour-infused baking spray

1. In medium bowl, beat together the butter and brown sugar until fluffy. Stir in the egg yolk. 2. Add the flour, white chocolate, baking soda, and vanilla and mix well. Stir in the chocolate crisps. 3. Line a 6-by-2-inch round baking pan with baking paper. Spray the baking paper with flour-infused baking spray. 4. Insert the crisper plate into the basket and the basket into the unit. Preheat the unit to 150ºC. 5. Spread the batter into the prepared pan, leaving a ½-inch border on all sides. 6. Once the unit is preheated, place the pan into the basket. 7. In zone 1, select the BAKE button, and set time to 9 minutes. In zone 2, select Match Cook and press Start. 8. When the cooking is complete, the cookies should be light brown and just barely set. Remove the pan from the basket and let cool for 10 minutes. Remove the biscuit from the pan, remove the baking paper, and let cool completely on a wire rack.

Chocolate Chip Biscuit Cake

Prep time: 5 minutes | Cook time: 15 minutes | Serves 8

- 4 tablespoons salted butter, melted
- 65 g granular brown sweetener
- 1 large egg
- ½ teaspoon vanilla extract
- 55 g blanched finely ground almond flour
- ½ teaspoon baking powder
- 40 g low-carb chocolate crisps

1. In a large bowl, whisk together butter, sweetener, egg, and vanilla. Add flour and baking powder and stir until combined. 2. Fold in chocolate crisps, then spoon batter into an ungreased round nonstick baking dish. 3. Place dish into air fryer basket. In zone 1, select the AIR FRY button, adjust temperature to 150ºC, set time to 15 minutes. In zone 2, select Match Cook and press Start. When edges are browned, biscuit cake will be done. 4. Slice and serve warm.

Pumpkin-Spice Bread Pudding

Prep time: 15 minutes | Cook time: 35 minutes | Serves 6

Bread Pudding:

- 175 ml heavy whipping cream
- 120 g canned pumpkin
- 80 ml whole milk
- 50 g granulated sugar
- 1 large egg plus 1 yolk
- ½ teaspoon pumpkin pie spice
- ⅛ teaspoon kosher, or coarse sea salt
- ⅓ loaf of day-old baguette or crusty country bread, cubed
- 4 tablespoons unsalted butter, melted

Sauce:

- 80 ml pure maple syrup
- 1 tablespoon unsalted butter
- 120 ml heavy whipping cream
- ½ teaspoon pure vanilla extract

1. For the bread pudding: In a medium bowl, combine the cream, pumpkin, milk, sugar, egg and yolk, pumpkin pie spice, and salt. Whisk until well combined. 2. In a large bowl, toss the bread cubes with the melted butter. Add the pumpkin mixture and gently toss until the ingredients are well combined. 3. Transfer the mixture to a baking pan. Place the pan in the air fryer basket. In zone 1, select the AIR FRY button, adjust temperature to 180ºC, set time to 35 minutes , or until custard is set in the middle. In zone 2, select Match Cook and press Start.4. Meanwhile, for the sauce: In a small saucepan, combine the syrup and butter. Heat over medium heat, stirring, until the butter melts. Stir in the cream and simmer, stirring often, until the sauce has thickened, about 15 minutes. Stir in the vanilla. Remove the pudding from the air fryer. 5. Let the pudding stand for 10 minutes before serving with the warm sauce.

Chocolate Cake

Prep time: 10 minutes | Cook time: 20 to 23 minutes | Serves 8

- 80 g granulated sugar
- 15 g Plain flour, plus 3 tablespoons
- 3 tablespoons cocoa
- ½ teaspoon baking powder
- ½ teaspoon baking soda
- ¼ teaspoon salt
- 1 egg
- 2 tablespoons oil
- 120 ml milk
- ½ teaspoon vanilla extract

1. Preheat the air fryer to 160ºC. 2. Grease and flour a baking pan. 3. In a medium bowl, stir together the sugar, flour, cocoa, baking powder, baking soda, and salt. 4. Add all other ingredients and beat with a wire whisk until smooth. 5. Pour batter into prepared pan and bake for 20 to 23 minutes, until toothpick inserted in center comes out clean, or with crumbs clinging to it.

Spiced Apple Cake

Prep time: 15 minutes | Cook time: 30 minutes | Serves 6

- Vegetable oil
- 2 diced & peeled Gala apples
- 1 tablespoon fresh lemon juice
- 55 g unsalted butter, softened
- 50 g granulated sugar
- 2 large eggs
- 80 g Plain flour
- 1½ teaspoons baking powder
- 1 tablespoon apple pie spice
- ½ teaspoon ground ginger
- ¼ teaspoon ground cardamom
- ¼ teaspoon ground nutmeg
- ½ teaspoon kosher, or coarse sea salt
- 60 ml whole milk
- Icing sugar, for dusting

1. Grease a 0.7-liter Bundt, or tube pan with oil; set aside. 2. In a medium bowl, toss the apples with the lemon juice until well coated; set aside. 3. In a large bowl, combine the butter and sugar. Beat with an electric hand mixer on medium speed until the sugar has dissolved. Add the eggs and beat until fluffy. Add the flour, baking powder, apple pie spice, ginger, cardamom, nutmeg, salt, and milk. Mix until the batter is thick but pourable. 4. Pour the batter into the prepared pan. Top batter evenly with the apple mixture. Place the pan in the air fryer basket. In zone 1, select the AIR FRY button, adjust temperature to 180ºC, set time to 30 minutes or until a toothpick inserted in the center of the cake comes out clean. In zone 2, select Match Cook and press Start. , Close the air fryer and let the cake rest for 10 minutes. Turn the cake out onto a wire rack and cool completely. 5. Right before serving, dust the cake with icing sugar.

Blackberry Cobbler

Prep time: 15 minutes | Cook time: 25 to 30 minutes | Serves 6

- 330 g fresh or frozen blackberries
- 260 g granulated sugar, divided into 200 g and 150 g
- 1 teaspoon vanilla extract
- 8 tablespoons butter, melted
- 65 g self-raising flour
- 1 to 2 tablespoons oil

1. In a medium bowl, stir together the blackberries, 200 g of sugar, and vanilla. 2. In another medium bowl, stir together the melted butter, remaining 150 g of sugar, and flour until a dough forms. 3. Spritz a baking pan with oil. Add the blackberry mixture. Crumble the flour mixture over the fruit. Cover the pan with aluminium foil. 4. Preheat the air fryer to 180ºC. 5. Place the covered pan in the air fryer basket. Cook for 20 to 25 minutes until the filling is thickened. 6. Uncover the pan and cook for 5 minutes more, depending on how juicy and browned you like your cobbler. Let sit for 5 minutes before serving.

Cinnamon and Pecan Pie

Prep time: 10 minutes | Cook time: 25 minutes | Serves 4

- 1 pack shortcrust pastry
- ½ teaspoons cinnamon
- ¾ teaspoon vanilla extract
- 2 eggs
- 175 ml maple syrup
- ⅛ teaspoon nutmeg
- 3 tablespoons melted butter, divided
- 2 tablespoons sugar
- 65 g chopped pecans

1. Preheat the air fryer to 190ºC. 2. In a small bowl, coat the pecans in 1 tablespoon of melted butter. 3. Transfer the pecans to the air fryer. In zone 1, select the AIR FRY button, and set time to 10 minutes. In zone 2, select Match Cook and press Start. 4. Put the pie dough in a greased pie dish, trim off the excess and add the pecans on top. 5. In a bowl, mix the rest of the ingredients. Pour this over the pecans. 6. Put the pan in the air fryer and bake for 25 minutes. 7. Serve immediately.

Chapter 9   Family Favorites

Coconut Chicken Tenders

Prep time: 10 minutes | Cook time: 12 minutes | Serves 4

- Oil, for spraying
- 2 large eggs
- 60 ml milk
- 1 tablespoon chilli sauce
- 350 g sweetened desiccated coconut
- 90 g Japanese breadcrumbs
- 1 teaspoon salt
- ½ teaspoon ground black pepper
- 450 g chicken tenders

1. Line the air fryer basket with parchment and spray lightly with oil. 2. In a small bowl, whisk together the eggs, milk, and chili sauce. 3. In a shallow dish, mix together the coconut, breadcrumbs, salt, and black pepper. 4. Coat the chicken in the egg mix, then dredge in the coconut mixture until evenly coated. 5. Place the chicken in the prepared basket and spray liberally with oil. 6. In zone 1, select the AIR FRY button, adjust temperature to 200ºC, set time to 6 minutes. In zone 2, select Match Cook and press Start. Flip, spray with more oil, and cook for another 6 minutes, or until the internal temperature reaches 74ºC.

Beef Jerky

Prep time: 30 minutes | Cook time: 2 hours | Serves 8

- Oil, for spraying
- 450 g silverside, cut into thin, short slices
- 60 ml soy sauce
- 3 tablespoons packed light muscovado sugar
- 1 tablespoon minced garlic
- 1 teaspoon ground ginger
- 1 tablespoon water

1. Line the air fryer basket with parchment and spray lightly with oil. 2. Place the steak, soy sauce, brown sugar, garlic, ginger, and water in a zip-top plastic bag, seal, and shake well until evenly coated. 3. Refrigerate for 30 minutes. Place the steak in the prepared basket in a single layer. 4. In zone 1, select the AIR FRY button, adjust temperature to 80ºC, set time to 120 minutes. In zone 2, select Match Cook and press Start. 6. Add more time if you like your jerky a bit tougher.

Churro Bites

Prep time: 5 minutes | Cook time: 6 minutes | Makes 36 bites

- Oil, for spraying
- 1 (500 g) package frozen puffed pastry, thawed
- 180 g caster sugar
- 1 tablespoon ground cinnamon
- 90 g icing sugar
- 1 tablespoon milk

1. Preheat the air fryer to 200ºC. 2.Line the air fryer basket with parchment and spray lightly with oil. 3.Unfold the puff pastry onto a clean work surface. Using a sharp knife, cut the dough into 36 bite-size pieces. 4.Place the dough pieces in one layer in the prepared basket, taking care not to let the pieces touch or overlap. 5. In zone 1, select the AIR FRY button, and set time to 3 minutes. In zone 2, select Match Cook and press Start. Flip, and cook for another 3 minutes, or until puffed and golden. In a small bowl, mix together the caster sugar and cinnamon. 6.In another small bowl, whisk together the icing sugar and milk. 7.Dredge the bites in the cinnamon-sugar mixture until evenly coated. 8.Serve with the icing on the side for dipping.

Old Bay Tilapia

Prep time: 15 minutes | Cook time: 6 minutes | Serves 4

- Oil, for spraying
- 235 ml panko breadcrumbs
- 2 tablespoons Old Bay or all-purpose seasoning
- 2 teaspoons granulated garlic
- 1 teaspoon onion powder
- ½ teaspoon salt
- ¼ teaspoon freshly ground black pepper
- 1 large egg
- 4 tilapia fillets

Preheat the air fryer to 204ºC. Line the air fryer basket with parchment and spray lightly with oil. 2. In a shallow bowl, mix together the breadcrumbs, seasoning, garlic, onion powder, salt, and black pepper. 3. In a small bowl, whisk the egg. Coat the tilapia in the egg, then dredge in the bread crumb mixture until completely coated. 4. Place the tilapia in the prepared basket. 5. Spray lightly with oil. In zone 1, select the AIR FRY button, and set time to 4 to 6 minutes , depending on the thickness of the fillets, until the internal temperature reaches 64ºC. In zone 2, select Match Cook and press Start.6. Serve immediately.

Cajun Shrimp

Prep time: 15 minutes | Cook time: 9 minutes | Serves 4

- Oil, for spraying
- 450 g king prawns, peeled and deveined
- 1 tablespoon Cajun seasoning
- 170 g Polish banger, cut into thick slices
- ½ medium courgette, cut into ¼-inch-thick slices
- ½ medium yellow marrow or butternut marrow, cut into ¼-inch-thick slices
- 1 green pepper, seeded and cut into 1-inch pieces
- 2 tablespoons olive oil
- ½ teaspoon salt

1. Preheat the air fryer to 200ºC. 2. Line the air fryer basket with parchment and spray lightly with oil. In a large bowl, toss together the shrimp and Cajun seasoning. 3. Add the kielbasa, courgette, marrow, pepper, olive oil, and salt and mix well. 4. Transfer the mixture to the prepared basket, taking care not to overcrowd. 5. In zone 1, select the AIR FRY button, and set time to 9 minutes. In zone 2, select Match Cook and press Start, shaking and stirring every 3 minutes. 7. Serve immediately.

Apple Pie Egg Rolls

Prep time: 10 minutes | Cook time: 8 minutes | Makes 6 rolls

- Oil, for spraying
- 1 (600 g) tin apple pie filling
- 1 tablespoon plain flour
- ½ teaspoon lemon juice
- ¼ teaspoon ground nutmeg
- ¼ teaspoon ground cinnamon
- 6 egg roll wrappers

1. Preheat the air fryer to 200ºC. 2. Line the air fryer basket with parchment and spray lightly with oil. 3. In a medium bowl, mix together the pie filling, flour, lemon juice, nutmeg, and cinnamon. 4. Lay out the egg roll wrappers on a work surface and spoon a dollop of pie filling in the centre of each. 5. Fill a small bowl with water. Dip your finger in the water and, working one at a time, moisten the edges of the wrappers. 6. Fold the wrapper like an packet: First fold one corner into the centre. 7. Fold each side corner in, and then fold over the remaining corner, making sure each corner overlaps a bit and the moistened edges stay closed. 8. Use additional water and your fingers to seal any open edges. 9. Place the rolls in the prepared basket and spray liberally with oil. 10. In zone 1, select the AIR FRY button, and set time to 4 minutes. In zone 2, select Match Cook and press Start. Flip, spray with oil, and cook for another 4 minutes, or until crispy and golden brown. 11. Serve immediately.

Meringue Cookies

Prep time: 15 minutes | Cook time: 1 hour 30 minutes | Makes 20 cookies

- Oil, for spraying
- 4 large egg whites
- 185 g sugar
- Pinch cream of tartar

1. Preheat the air fryer to 60ºC. 2.Line the air fryer basket with parchment and spray lightly with oil. 3.In a small heatproof bowl, whisk together the egg whites and sugar. 4.Fill a small saucepan halfway with water, place it over medium heat, and bring to a light simmer. 5.Place the bowl with the egg whites on the saucepan, making sure the bottom of the bowl does not touch the water. 6.Whisk the mixture until the sugar is dissolved. Transfer the mixture to a large bowl and add the cream of tartar. 7.Using an electric mixer, beat the mixture on high until it is glossy and stiff peaks form. 8.Transfer the mixture to a piping bag or a zip-top plastic bag with a corner cut off. Pipe rounds into the prepared basket. 9. In zone 1, select the AIR FRY button, and set time to 90 minutes. In zone 2, select Match Cook and press Start. 10.Turn off the air fryer and let the meringues cool completely inside. 11.The residual heat will continue to dry them out.

Meatball Subs

Prep time: 15 minutes | Cook time: 19 minutes | Serves 6

- Oil, for spraying
- 450 g 15% fat minced beef
- 120 ml Italian breadcrumbs (mixed breadcrumbs, Italian seasoning and salt)
- 1 tablespoon dried minced onion
- 1 tablespoon minced garlic
- 1 large egg
- 1 teaspoon salt
- 1 teaspoon freshly ground black pepper
- 6 sub rolls
- 1 (510 g) jar marinara sauce
- 350 ml shredded Mozzarella cheese

1. Line the air fryer basket with parchment and spray lightly with oil. 2. In a large bowl, mix together the ground beef, bread crumbs, onion, garlic, egg, salt, and black pepper. Roll the mixture into 18 meatballs. 3. Place the meatballs in the prepared basket. 4. In zone 1, select the AIR FRY button, adjust temperature to 199ºC, set time to 5 minutes. In zone 2, select Match Cook and press Start. 5. Place 3 meatballs in each hoagie roll. Top with marinara and Mozzarella cheese. 6. Place the loaded rolls in the air fryer and cook for 3 to 4 minutes, or until the cheese is melted. Serve immediately.

Pork Stuffing Meatballs

Prep time: 10 minutes | Cook time: 12 minutes | Makes 35 meatballs

- Oil, for spraying
- 680 g finely chopped pork
- 120 g breadcrumbs
- 120 ml milk
- 60 g finely chopped onion
- 1 large egg
- 1 tablespoon dried rosemary
- 1 tablespoon dried thyme
- 1 teaspoon salt
- 1 teaspoon ground black pepper
- 1 teaspoon finely chopped fresh parsley

1. Line the air fryer basket with parchment and spray lightly with oil. 2.In a large bowl, mix together the finely chopped pork, breadcrumbs, milk, onion, egg, rosemary, thyme, salt, black pepper, and parsley. 3.Roll about 2 tablespoons of the mixture into a ball. 4.Repeat with the rest of the mixture. You should have 30 to 35 meatballs. 5.Place the meatballs in the prepared basket in a single layer, leaving space between each one.6. In zone 1, select the AIR FRY button, adjust temperature to 200°C, set time to 10 to 12 minutes. In zone 2, select Match Cook and press Start, flipping after 5 minutes, or until golden brown and the internal temperature reaches 72°C.

Puffed Egg Tarts

Prep time: 10 minutes | Cook time: 42 minutes | Makes 4 tarts

- Oil, for spraying
- Plain flour, for dusting
- 1 (340 g) sheet frozen puff pastry, thawed
- 180 g shredded Cheddar cheese, divided
- 4 large eggs
- 2 teaspoons chopped fresh parsley
- Salt and ground black pepper, to taste

1. Preheat the air fryer to 200°C. 2.Line the air fryer basket with parchment and spray lightly with oil. Lightly dust your work surface with flour. 3.Unfold the puff pastry and cut it into 4 equal squares. 4.Place 2 squares in the prepared basket. Cook for 10 minutes. 5.Remove the basket. Press the centre of each tart shell with a spoon to make an indentation. 6.Sprinkle 3 tablespoons of cheese into each indentation and crack 1 egg into the centre of each tart shell. 7. In zone 1, select the AIR FRY button, and set time to 7 to 11 minutes , or until the eggs are cooked to your desired doneness. In zone 2, select Match Cook and press Start.8.Sprinkle evenly with the parsley, and season with salt and black pepper. 9.Serve immediately.

Chapter 10   Fast and Easy Everyday Favourites

Cheesy Chilli Toast

Prep time: 5 minutes | Cook time: 5 minutes | Serves 1

- 2 tablespoons grated Parmesan cheese
- 2 tablespoons grated Mozzarella cheese
- 2 teaspoons salted butter, at room temperature
- 10 to 15 thin slices serrano chilli or jalapeño
- 2 slices sourdough bread
- ½ teaspoon black pepper

1. Preheat the air fryer to 160ºC. 2.In a small bowl, stir together the Parmesan, Mozzarella, butter, and chillies. 3.Spread half the mixture onto one side of each slice of bread. 4.Sprinkle with the pepper. 5.Place the slices, cheese-side up, in the air fryer basket. 6. In zone 1, select the BAKE button, and set time to 5 minutes., or until the cheese has melted and started to brown slightly. In zone 2, select Match Cook and press Start7.Serve immediately.

Cheesy Baked Coarse Cornmeal

Prep time: 10 minutes | Cook time: 12 minutes | Serves 6

- 180 ml hot water
- 2 (28 g) packages instant grits
- 1 large egg, beaten
- 1 tablespoon melted butter
- 2 cloves garlic, minced
- ½ to 1 teaspoon red pepper flakes
- 235 g shredded Cheddar cheese or jalapeño Jack cheese

1. Preheat the air fryer to 200ºC. 2.In a baking tray, combine the water, coarse cornmeal, egg, butter, garlic, and red pepper flakes. Stir until well combined. 3.Stir in the shredded cheese. 4.Place the pan in the air fryer basket and air fry for 12 minutes, or until the coarse cornmeal have cooked through and a knife inserted near the centre comes out clean. 5.Let stand for 5 minutes before serving.

Beetroot Salad with Lemon Vinaigrette

Prep time: 10 minutes | Cook time: 12 to 15 minutes | Serves 4

- 6 medium red and golden beetroots, peeled and sliced
- 1 teaspoon olive oil
- ¼ teaspoon rock salt
- 2 teaspoons olive oil
- 2 tablespoons chopped fresh chives
- 120 g crumbled feta cheese
- 2 kg mixed greens
- Cooking spray

Vinaigrette:
- Juice of 1 lemon

1. Preheat the air fryer to 180ºC. 2. In a large bowl, toss the beetroots, olive oil, and rock salt. 3. Spray the air fryer basket with cooking spray, then place the beetroots in the basket. In zone 1, select the AIR FRY button, and set time to 12 to 15 minutes or until tender. In zone 2, select Match Cook and press Start. 4. While the beetroots cook, make the vinaigrette in a large bowl by whisking together the olive oil, lemon juice, and chives. 5. Remove the beetroots from the air fryer, toss in the vinaigrette, and allow to cool for 5 minutes. 6. Add the feta and serve on top of the mixed greens.

Air Fried Butternut Marrow with Chopped Hazelnuts

Prep time: 10 minutes | Cook time: 20 minutes | Makes 700 ml

- 2 tablespoons whole hazelnuts
- 700 g butternut marrow, peeled, deseeded, and cubed
- ¼ teaspoon rock salt
- ¼ teaspoon freshly ground black pepper
- 2 teaspoons olive oil
- Cooking spray

1. Preheat the air fryer to 150ºC. 2. Spritz the air fryer basket with cooking spray. 3. Arrange the hazelnuts in the preheated air fryer. Air fry for 3 minutes or until soft. 4. Chopped the hazelnuts roughly and transfer to a small bowl. Set aside. 5. In zone 1, select the AIR FRY button, adjust temperature to 180ºC, set time to 20 minutes. In zone 2, select Match Cook and press Start. 6. Spritz with cooking spray. Put the butternut marrow in a large bowl, then sprinkle with salt and pepper and drizzle with olive oil. 7. Toss to coat well. Transfer the marrow in the air fryer. 8. Shake the basket halfway through the frying time. 9. When the frying is complete, transfer the marrow onto a plate and sprinkle with chopped hazelnuts before serving.

Bacon Pinwheels

Prep time: 10 minutes | Cook time: 10 minutes | Makes 8 pinwheels

- 1 sheet puff pastry
- 2 tablespoons maple syrup
- 48 g brown sugar
- 8 slices bacon
- Ground black pepper, to taste
- Cooking spray

1. Preheat the air fryer to 180ºC. 2. Spritz the air fryer basket with cooking spray. 3. Roll the puff pastry into a 10-inch square with a rolling pin on a clean work surface, then cut the pastry into 8 strips. 4. Brush the strips with maple syrup and sprinkle with sugar, leaving a 1-inch far end uncovered. 5. Arrange each slice of bacon on each strip, leaving a ⅛-inch length of bacon hang over the end close to you. Sprinkle with black pepper. 6. From the end close to you, roll the strips into pinwheels, then dab the uncovered end with water and seal the rolls. 7. Arrange the pinwheels in the preheated air fryer and spritz with cooking spray. 8. In zone 1, select the AIR FRY button, and set time to 10 minutes or until golden brown. In zone 2, select Match Cook and press Start. 9. Flip the pinwheels halfway through. 10. Serve immediately.

Air Fried Tortilla Chips

Prep time: 5 minutes | Cook time: 10 minutes | Serves 4

- 4 six-inch corn tortillas, cut in half and slice into thirds
- 1 tablespoon rapeseed oil
- ¼ teaspoon rock salt
- Cooking spray

1. Preheat the air fryer to 180ºC. 2.Spritz the air fryer basket with cooking spray. 3.On a clean work surface, brush the tortilla chips with rapeseed oil, then transfer the chips in the preheated air fryer. 4. In zone 1, select the AIR FRY button, and set time to 10 minutes or until crunchy and lightly browned. In zone 2, select Match Cook and press Start. 5.Shake the basket and sprinkle with salt halfway through the cooking time. 6.Transfer the chips onto a plate lined with paper towels. 7.Serve immediately.

Corn Fritters

Prep time: 15 minutes | Cook time: 8 minutes | Serves 6

- 120 g self-raising flour
- 1 tablespoon sugar
- 1 teaspoon salt
- 1 large egg, lightly beaten
- 60 g buttermilk
- 180 g corn kernels
- 60 g minced onion
- Cooking spray

1. Preheat the air fryer to 180°C. 2.Line the air fryer basket with parchment paper. In a medium bowl, whisk the flour, sugar, and salt until blended. Stir in the egg and buttermilk. 3.Add the corn and minced onion. 4.Mix well. Shape the corn fritter batter into 12 balls. 5.Place the fritters on the parchment and spritz with oil. In zone 1, select the BAKE button, and set time to 4 minutes. In zone 2, select Match Cook and press Start. 6.Flip the fritters, spritz them with oil, and bake for 4 minutes more until firm and lightly browned. 7.Serve immediately.

Traditional Queso Fundido

Prep time: 10 minutes | Cook time: 25 minutes | Serves 4

- 110 g fresh Mexican (or Spanish if unavailable) chorizo, casings removed
- 1 medium onion, chopped
- 3 cloves garlic, minced
- 235 g chopped tomato
- 2 jalapeños, deseeded and diced
- 2 teaspoons ground cumin
- 475 g shredded Oaxaca or Mozzarella cheese
- 120 ml half-and-half (60 g whole milk and 60 ml cream combined)
- Celery sticks or tortilla chips, for serving

1. Preheat the air fryer to 200°C. 2.In a baking tray, combine the chorizo, onion, garlic, tomato, jalapeños, and cumin. Stir to combine. 3.Place the pan in the air fryer basket. 4.Air fry for 15 minutes, or until the banger is cooked, stirring halfway through the cooking time to break up the banger. 5.Add the cheese and half-and-half; stir to combine. 6.Air fry for 10 minutes, or until the cheese has melted. 7.Serve with celery sticks or maize wrap chips.

Sweet Maize and Carrot Fritters

Prep time: 10 minutes | Cook time: 8 to 11 minutes | Serves 4

- 1 medium-sized carrot, grated
- 1 brown onion, finely chopped
- 4 ounces (113 g) canned sweet maize kernels, drained
- 1 teaspoon sea salt flakes
- 1 tablespoon chopped fresh coriander
- 1 medium-sized egg, whisked
- 2 tablespoons plain milk
- 1 cup grated Parmesan cheese
- ¼ cup flour
- ⅓ teaspoon baking powder
- ⅓ teaspoon sugar
- Cooking spray

1. Preheat the air fryer to 350ºF (177ºC). 2. Place the grated carrot in a colander and press down to squeeze out any excess moisture. Dry it with a paper towel. 3. Combine the carrots with the remaining ingredients. 4. Mold 1 tablespoon of the mixture into a ball and press it down with your hand or a spoon to flatten it. Repeat until the rest of the mixture is used up. 5. Spritz the balls with cooking spray. 6. Arrange in the air fryer basket, taking care not to overlap any balls. In zone 1, select the BAKE button, and set time to 8 t0 11 minutes , or until they're firm. In zone 2, select Match Cook and press Start. 7. Serve warm.

Beery and Crunchy Onion Rings

Prep time: 10 minutes | Cook time: 16 minutes | Serves 2 to 4

- 80 g plain flour
- 1 teaspoon paprika
- ½ teaspoon bicarbonate of soda
- 1 teaspoon salt
- ½ teaspoon freshly ground black pepper
- 1 egg, beaten
- 180 ml beer
- 175 g breadcrumbs
- 1 tablespoons olive oil
- 1 large Vidalia or sweet onion, peeled and sliced into ½-inch rings
- Cooking spray

1. Preheat the air fryer to 180ºC. Spritz the air fryer basket with cooking spray. 2. Combine the flour, paprika, bicarbonate of soda, salt, and ground black pepper in a bowl. Stir to mix well. 3. Combine the egg and beer in a separate bowl. Stir to mix well. 4 Make a well in the centre of the flour mixture, then pour the egg mixture in the well. Stir to mix everything well. 5. Pour the breadcrumbs and olive oil in a shallow plate. Stir to mix well. 6. Dredge the onion rings gently into the flour and egg mixture, then shake the excess off and put into the plate of breadcrumbs. 7. Flip to coat both sides well. 8 Arrange the onion rings in the preheated air fryer. In zone 1, select the AIR FRY button, and set time to 16 minutes or until golden brown and crunchy. In zone 2, select Match Cook and press Start.9. Flip the rings and put the bottom rings to the top halfway through. Serve immediately.

Appendix : Recipes Index

A

Air Fried Butternut Marrow with	70
Air Fried Tortilla Chips	71
Almond and Caraway Crust Steak	28
Almond-Crusted Fish	39
Apple Pie Egg Rolls	66
Apple Rolls	9
Asian Tofu Salad	16

B

Bacon and Cheese Stuffed Pork Chops	24
Bacon Cheese Egg with Avocado	4
Bacon Pinwheels	71
Banger-Stuffed Mushroom Caps	11
Beef Jerky	64
Beery and Crunchy Onion Rings	73
Beetroot Salad with Lemon Vinaigrette	70
Berry Muffins	6
Black Cod with Grapes and Kale	40
Blackberry Cobbler	63
Blackened Fish	43
Blackened Red Snapper	40
Browned Prawns Patties	39
Browned Ricotta with Capers and Lemon	52
Bunless Breakfast Turkey Burgers	5
Butter and Garlic Fried Cabbage	17

C

Cajun Bacon Pork Loin Fillet	24
Cajun Shrimp	66
Caprese Aubergine Stacks	23
Caramelized Aubergine with Harissa Yoghurt	15
Caramelized Fruit Skewers	59
Celery Chicken	44
Cheddar Eggs	8
Cheese Drops	53
Cheese Pork Chops	33
Cheese Stuffed Courgette	23
Cheese-Encrusted Chicken Tenderloins with Peanuts	51
Cheesy Baked Coarse Cornmeal	69
Cheesy Chilli Toast	69
Cheesy Loaded Broccoli	11
Cheesy Steak Fries	58
Chicken Legs with Leeks	48
Chicken Pesto Pizzas	49
Chicken Rochambeau	50
Chicken Thighs in Waffles	47
Chilli Lime Prawns	41
Chilli-brined Fried Calamari	56
Chimichanga Breakfast Burrito	6
Chocolate Bread Pudding	60
Chocolate Cake	62
Chocolate Chip Biscuit Cake	61
Chopped Hazelnuts	70
Chorizo and Beef Burger	25
Churro Bites	65
Cinnamon and Pecan Pie	63
Citrus-Roasted Broccoli Florets	18
Classic Fish Fingers with Tartar Sauce	43
Coconut Chicken Tenders	64
Cod with Avocado	34
Corn Fritters	72
Crab Cake Sandwich	36
Cranberry Curry Chicken	50
Cream-Filled Sponge Cakes	59
Crispy Aubergine Rounds	20
Curried Orange Honey Chicken	45

D

Dark Chocolate and Cranberry Muesli Bars	52
Deconstructed Chicago Dogs	32
Drop Biscuits	4

E

Easy Chicken Fingers	51
Egg in a Hole	9

F

Fish Croquettes with Lemon-Dill Aioli	35
Fried Brussels Sprouts	15

G

Garlic and Thyme Tomatoes	18
Garlic Butter Prawns Scampi	37
Garlic Lemon Scallops	38
Garlic Parmesan Drumsticks	47

Garlic-Parmesan Crispy Baby Potatoes	14
Glazed Carrots	14
Golden Onion Rings	54
Golden Tenders	49
Greek Stuffed Aubergine	22

H

Herbed Shiitake Mushrooms	17

I

Italian Banger Links	27

K

Keto Quiche	5
Kheema Burgers	30

L

Lamb and Cucumber Burgers	29
Lemon-Pepper Trout	37
Lemony Endive in Curried Yoghurt	55
Loaded Cauliflower Steak	22
Lush Chocolate Chip Cookies	60

M

Meatball Subs	67
Mediterranean Pan Pizza	21
Meringue Cookies	67
Meritage Eggs	10
Mexican Potato Skins	57
Mojito Lamb Chops	26
Mozzarella Bacon Calzones	8

N

Nigerian Peanut-Crusted Bavette Steak	27

O

Old Bay Tilapia	65
Oyster Po'Boy	41

P

Panko Crusted Calf's Liver Strips	32
Parmesan and Herb Sweet Potatoes	13
Parmesan Herb Focaccia Bread	12
Pepper Stuffed Chicken Roll-Ups	46
Pizza Eggs	7
Pork and Pinto Bean Gorditas	25
Pork Loin Roast	31
Pork Stuffing Meatballs	68
Puffed Egg Tarts	68
Pumpkin-Spice Bread Pudding	61

R

Red Pepper Tapenade	56
Roasted Mushrooms with Garlic	54
Roasted Pearl Onion Dip	53
Roasted Salmon Fillets	38
Roasted Vegetable Mélange with Herbs	19
Roasted Vegetables with Rice	19

S

Salmon Fritters with Courgette	34
Sesame Chicken Breast	48
Shishito Pepper Roast	13
Shishito Peppers with Herb Dressing	57
Sichuan Cumin Lamb	33
Sirloin Steak with Honey-Mustard Butter	29
Snapper Scampi	36
Snapper with Shallot and Tomato	42
South Indian Pepper Chicken	46
Spanish Chicken and Mini Sweet Pepper Baguette	45
Spiced Apple Cake	62
Spicy Lamb Sirloin Chops	28
Spinach and Sweet Pepper Poppers	12
Spinach and Swiss Frittata with Mushrooms	10
Steak with Pepper	26
Steak, Broccoli, and Mushroom Rice Bowls	31
Stuffed Fried Mushrooms	58
Stuffed Portobellos	21
Sweet Maize and Carrot Fritters	73
Sweet Tilapia Fillets	35

T

Tahini-Lemon Kale	16
Tangy Fried A Gherkin Spears	55
Teriyaki Cauliflower	20
Three-Berry Dutch Pancake	7
Traditional Queso Fundido	72
Tuna with Herbs	42
Turkish Chicken Kebabs	44
Tuscan Air Fried Veal Loin	30

Printed in Great Britain
by Amazon